DRESSED to KILL

DRESSED to KILL

Cartoonists and the
Northern Ireland
Conflict

Foreword by
Martyn Turner

John Darby

Appletree
Press

First published and printed by
The Appletree Press Ltd
7 James Street South
Belfast BT2 8DL
1983

British Library Cataloguing in Publication Data
Darby, John
    Dressed to kill: cartoonists and the Northern
Ireland conflict.
    1. Northern Ireland—Politics and government
    2. Northern Ireland—History—1969-
    I. Title
    941.60824   DA990.U6

ISBN 0-904651-91-6

to Patrick and Michael

Contents

Acknowledgments

Grateful acknowledgment is made to the following for permission to reproduce cartoons:

The *Arizona Republic*, for the cartoon by Steve Benson; the cartoonist and the *Chicago Tribune*, for the cartoon by Wayne Stayskal; the cartoonist, for the cartoon by Jim Fitzpatrick; the cartoonist, for cartoons by Rowel Friers; the cartoonist and *Information on Ireland*, for the cartoon by Bill Sanderson; the cartoonist, the *Irish Independent* and the *Irish Press*, for cartoons by Doll; the cartoonists and the *Irish Times*, for the cartoons by Drake and Ged; the cartoonist and *The Listener*, for the cartoon by Barry Fantoni; the cartoonist and *The Philadelphia Inquirer*, for the cartoon by Auth; the cartoonists and *Private Eye*, for cartoons by Austin, Dredge and McLachlan; the cartoonists and *Fortnight*, for cartoons by Martyn Turner and Dobson; the cartoonists and the *Spectator*, for cartoons by Cummings, Heath and Richard Willson; the cartoonist and *Loyalist News*, for the cartoon by Rab the cartoonist and *Republican News*, for cartoons by Cormac; the cartoonist and the *Guardian*, for the cartoon by Gibbard; the cartoonist and the *Andersonstown News*, for cartoons by Oisin; the cartoonist and *Visor*, for cartoons by Carr and Nicale; the cartoonist and the *Sunday Tribune*, for the cartoons by Quinn; the cartoonists and *Punch*, for cartoons by Cookson, 'EM', David Langdon, Mahood, De la Nongerede, Raymond, Trog and Mike Williams; Universal Press Syndicate, for the cartoon by Oliphant; the cartoonist and the *Observer* for cartoons by Trog; the cartoonists and the *New Statesman*, for cartoons by Horner, Thompson and Wheeler; the cartoonists and the *Sunday Times*, for cartoons by Calman and Scarfe; the cartoonist and the *Daily Express*, for the cartoon by Cummings; the editor of *Police Beat*; the editor of *Socialist Challenge*, the Ulster Defence Association; and the National Library of Ireland.

Foreword

To be forewarded is to be forearmed. This is a non-governmental health warning about cartoonists and their motives, and about a few of the ways in which the cartoonist's motives and insights can be distorted before his work reaches the printed page. Political cartoonists may be seen as reformers and as the little boy who shouts that the emperor has no clothes. I just want to point out, to be fair and cynical, that sometimes the little boy isn't wearing very much either.

In my limited experience, corroborated by Hewison (art editor of *Punch* and author of *The Cartoon Connection*), wherever professional cartoonists gather the talk is of one thing—money. I would extend that to say that wherever professional artists of any kind gather (novelists, sculptors, musicians) the talk is always of how to earn a living and how rotten it is that we have to spend all our free time talking about money. The last letter I got from a friend of literary persuasion said approximately: 'Have sold a play to the BBC, they are planning to pay me £1,535, and sixpence. PS. I would like your opinion on the enclosed.'

In Ireland, for the cartoonist, the 'money rules' rule is especially true, for in Ireland the cartoonist is an endangered species. Thus the first thing to bear in mind is that, contrary to public opinion, a cartoon published in a national newspaper does not equate to a pension for life and that the prime motivation of any cartoonist trying to make a living out of his work is to get something, anything, published. Thus in the twilight zone of Dublin cartooning, young bearded gentlemen can be observed knocking out big-booted heavy squad police brutality cartoons with one hand while fulfilling a regular obligation for a regular fee to a garda journal with the other.

In terms of political cartooning the economic way of the world leads to a sort of life cycle within life. The would-be cartoonist, full of political ideas and ways to change the world, starts out. He is keen and eager and probably a student, or employed in some none too rigorous occupation that leaves him time for much thinking and a little drawing. He is able to say exactly what he wants and then to go and find a publisher. If he fails to find anyone willing to publish he can either carry on being a student/clerk/bus conductor/whatever or he can move on to the second phase of cartooning. The second phase consists of tailoring your output to meet the market needs. Some, on reaching this phase, change from political to social cartooning and sign their work 'Sprod' or 'Bif' and develop an interest in mothers-in-law, washing lines and jungle animals, and settle for a quiet life sending great wads of work from magazine to magazine while still, occasionally, attempting to interest editors in their real work.

Many of the world's most successful political cartoonists go through this phase in a slightly revised manner. If they are lucky enough to get a regular outlet in a national newspaper or magazine they attempt to survive a period of time during which the editor's boat should not be rocked. This is the stage when the would-be cartoonist should slowly change from being 'the cartoonist' to being 'the Fred Bloggs'.

'The Fred Bloggs' is allowed a degree of freedom of expression that might be denied to 'the cartoonist'. A point has been reached when the cartoon is often identified with the cartoonist rather than with the paper. It is a Fred Bloggs cartoon in the *Daily Blag* rather than a *Daily Blag* cartoon.

But even if this stage has been attained the Fred Bloggs is subject to other constraints. While latitude is allowed editorially, it does not give any cartoonist carte-blanche. Even Ronald Searle's definitive collection is scattered with unpublished work as are most other cartoonists collections (including my own, now on sale).

In Britain and America, where newspapers employ editorial cartoonists, the general rule is that the cartoonist waylays the editor early in the day with a few roughs of ideas for the next day. The usual form is to think of one idea and then produce a few others so excruciatingly bad that even the average visually illiterate editor can pick the right one to be drawn properly for publication. Unfortunately, so I am told, this system occasionally breaks down, which explains why a percentage of cartoons are not worth publishing. The other reason, of course, is that it just isn't possible to be wordly wise, witty and rapier-like every day of the week over a long period of time.

This system does not apply with my own paper, the *Irish Times*, an enlightened and thinking organ. On the one occasion I happened to be in the office and felt under an obligation to produce a cartoon I thought I would try the method of selection described above so I could find out what it felt like to be a real cartoonist. I drew three roughs and went in search of the editor. He looked at them. 'Do them all,' he said. I have never repeated the experiment.

Thus expression is limited by economics and by editors. The third limitation is public opinion and public knowledge. It has been said to me, frequently, that I must read an awful lot to get ideas for cartoons. 'No,' I reply, 'I just read the sports page and see what's on television just like everyone else. I sort of glance through the rest.' Cartoonists work off headlines and really have to work within that rigid framework. Thus even if I care deeply and profoundly about a particular subject, I can't get these feelings out of the way and onto paper unless there is a current hook to hang it on. One doesn't lose interest in subjects, the subjects merely become less interesting to the media. While Carnsore Point was an issue in Irish politics I was able to produce a whole sheaf of cartoons about the evils of nuclear power (and even an article). Now it's no longer an issue so I don't draw cartoons about it. But that doesn't mean I feel less strongly about it.

The fourth and final limitation is a personal one. Somewhere in this learned tome reference is made to the small amount of work I now produce on Northern Ireland. It is strange when you consider that it remains the main story in Irish politics. Well, here in Dublin it isn't much of an issue at all. I remember an *Irish Times* editorial rightly saying that it was dreadful to think that the death of a Garda in Wexford is headline news in our papers for weeks whereas the death of an RUC man in Armagh rates a paragraph at the bottom of page five. That is, however, a true reflection of the republicanism of the Republic. Thus I respond, in a way, to the market—no interest, no cartoons (especially when the readership wouldn't understand the local niceties of the Belfast situation).

Furthermore, I don't feel comfortable pontificating on a life-and-death situation from the comparative safety of Co. Kildare, where I now live. I wrote jokes about bombs and bombers for the BBC when I lived in the North. I wouldn't feel I had the right to do that from my armchair down here. Also after almost a decade of writing and drawing about the North I have pretty well said all there is to be said. In fact I had pretty well said it all after the first cartoon. The philosophy is simple: 'some things might be worth dying for, nothing is worth killing for.'

Martyn Turner
July 1983

Introduction

Randall Harrison, in his book *The Cartoon*, recounts a popular anecdote about cartoonists. It concerned a publisher who complained to a cartoonist about paying $100 for a cartoon which consisted of only four lines. 'Obviously you do not understand my art,' replied the cartoonist. 'If I could have done it in three lines, the price would have been $1000.'

To anyone interested in the analysis of cartoons, this comes close to explaining their unique quality. The appeal lies in their very lack of adornment. Many cartoonists have commented on this. Michael Cummings explained it like this: 'As a little boy one was told it was rude to stare or to mock people's features. This is the first thing a cartoonist does, like a rude little boy going around making occasional farting noises with his mouth' (Wynn Jones 1971). Osbert Lancaster was also attracted by the comparison with children: 'It is not the cartoonist's business to wave flags and cheer as the procession passes; his allotted role is that of the little boy who points out that the Emperor is stark naked' (*Drawn and Quartered* 1970). It has been observed that American cartoonists, almost unique among the Washington press corps, avoid socialising with politicians, in case their essential mixture of vitriol and humour might be diluted: 'They have no stake in cultivating sources; nothing could be less useful to a cartoonist than a secret' (*Newsweek* 1980). This independent status allows the cartoonist to get away with murder, or at any rate with comments which would have his reporter colleagues before the courts. Jeff MacNelly, the American cartoonist, believed that the results justified the indulgence:

> Political cartoonists violate every rule of political journalism—they misquote, trifle with the truth, make science fiction out of politics and sometimes should be held for personal libel. But when the smoke clears, the political cartoonist has been getting closer to the truth than the guys who write political opinions. (*Newsweek* 1980)

There is no doubt that such a permissive art form attracts a curious breed of practitioners. As MacNelly went on to add, there are 'many great cartoonists who, if they couldn't draw, would be hired assassins'.

The particular function of the political cartoonist is to render down complicated issues into a single essence. When it is done effectively, the power of a cartoon lies in its concentration and simplification, and in its ability to impress the memory more indelibly than columns of print. Herbloc's 1949 cartoon on right-wing fanaticism in the United States, for example, has these qualities; once seen, it is difficult to forget: Hysteria, clutching a bucket of water and crying 'Fire!', clambers up a ladder to douse a flame—but the flame is the torch of the statue of Liberty.

It is difficult to assess the extent to which public opinion was influenced by such cartoons, but there is no doubt about politicians' believing that they were. A drawing of Louis Philippe as Gargantua earned the nineteenth century cartoonist six months in a French prison; Thomas Nast was described by Abraham Lincoln as 'our best recruiting sergeant' during the American Civil war, and his cartoons of Boss Tweed, which eventually led to Tweed's imprisonment and overthrow as Democratic leader in New York, drew the remark from Tweed that he was unconcerned about hostile editorials because his constituents were illiterate, but 'them damn pictures...'; Hitler honoured David Low by placing him high on his list for liquidation after the conquest of Britain. Nor have the political fears diminished in recent years; in 1981 Francisco Pons, the Uraguayan political cartoonist, was still in prison for his skills.

Despite all this, interest in the study of cartoons is relatively new. The 1981 membership of the Association of American Editorial Cartoonists stood at around 170 members, almost twice the 1980 figure (Harrison 1981). In 1975 the University of Kent established a Centre for the Study of Cartoons—an event, incidently, which prompted this advice from *Punch*: 'The motives of cartoonists are one of the most important matters that the boys at Canterbury must investigate, and I have news for them. Most, nay all, cartoonists do it for the money' (Hardcastle 1975). These organisational changes have reflected a marked increase in the number of studies examining particular themes through the eyes of cartoonists. The Kennedy assassination (Rajski 1967), Watergate (Wheeler and Reed 1975), the role of women (Meyer et al. 1980), the American Presidency (Blaisdell and Selz 1976)—all have been the subject of recent research. A more recent study of political cartoons and cartoonists (*Newsweek* 1980), focussing on the 1980 Presidential campaign in the United States, argued that their importance was increasing; although there is still very little evidence on the impact of cartoons on readers' attitudes, the *Newsweek* survey demonstrated clearly that American politicians were convinced that it was considerable. Cartoons about Ireland too have attracted interest: *Punch*'s view of Ireland has been discussed by Price (1971), and a major study of the Irishman in Victorian caricature has been written by Curtis (1971). Some of these have been inspired by the suitability of cartoons for social comment, and others by cartoons as an art form.

This book is less concerned with the artistic merit of cartoons than with their ability to demonstrate different perceptions of the violence in Northern Ireland. It has two main objects, one general and one local.

The first is to examine the possibility of using political cartoons as a basis for political analysis of newspapers. The argument here is that cartoons not only reflect the political stance of the publication in which they are printed, but also, over a period of time, accurately reflect changes in editorial policy. Two factors support this contention: in the first place the very nature of political cartoons does not permit the cartoonist to qualify his main observation. Unlike his reporter colleagues, he cannot add conditional clauses, and must express his view in its most stark and uncompromising form; the concept of fair play has no place in cartoons. Add to that the fact that a cartoonist who disagrees with the political stance of his newspaper is unlikely to continue in print or in employment for long—indeed he is unlikely to have been employed in the first place. The Northern Irish conflict is an interesting case study of the relationships between cartoonists, their publications and the political system in which they operate.

At another level the book explores the insights provided into a decade of Northern Ireland's violence by cartoonists from different national and political backgrounds. Events in the province since 1969 were sufficiently newsworthy to produce thousands of political cartoons in many countries. These provide an unusually self-contained subject for analysis—long enough to detect how attitudes have changed, and broad enough for cross-national comparisons.

A variety of settings is examined. Chapter 1 deals with the historical treatment of the Irish by cartoonists, and introduces some themes which recur in the cartoons of the 1970s. Chapter 2 examines the large number of cartoons which appeared in British publications, and discusses some of the dilemmas they reveal. Cartoons in the mainstream Irish newspapers and magazines are the subject of Chapter 3, and Chapter 4 considers the cartoons which appeared in newspapers produced by the British army, and by republican and loyalist groups. Chapter 5 is devoted to cartoons which appeared outside the British Isles. Finally, Chapter 6 draws together some of the central themes in the book, including the constraints on cartoonists, and examines the relationship between cartoons and their setting.

The cartoons themselves are shown underneath the main text. These are grouped within fourteen sections, and each section has its own commentary, so that they may be examined independently, or in parallel with the main analysis.

Altogether the book is based on more than 3,000 cartoons about Northern Ireland which have been drawn since 1969. Most have appeared in the mainstream Irish and British newspapers and magazines. In all, eighteen publications from Belfast and Dublin, and seventeen London publications, have been examined systematically over the twelve-year period of study. Only a more intermittent study of the immense British underground press was possible.

An extra dimension is added by cartoons which have appeared in the publications of loyalist and republican organisations, and of the British army. Some of these newspapers have had short life spans, but all issues of eleven publications have been examined comprehensively.

The examination of overseas cartoons created greater problems. It is clearly impossible to attempt a systematic survey of them. Nevertheless they provide important insights into how the conflict was regarded abroad. The published indexes for some papers, notably *Pravda*, indicate the themes of political cartoons, but in most cases I am indebted to friends and colleagues in different countries, whose diligent monitoring of their newspapers made it possible to gain some impression of how the issue was treated abroad. Although not all have been reproduced, more than fifty cartoons have been examined from the United States, Canada, South Africa, Australia, the Soviet Union, India, Greece, France, Germany, Holland and the Scandanavian countries. Whether they are representative of the press in general must remain a question. They only provide a taste, not a meal.

The historical chapter is greatly in debt to the excellent books by Curtis (1971) and Lebow (1976). These have been supplemented by personal research into the treatment by cartoonists of particular periods, notably the Famine years and the Ulster crisis from 1886 to 1925.

Many thanks are due to many people: to the Research Committee of the New University of Ulster for financial assistance towards the project; to my friends and colleagues who monitored the overseas press on my behalf; to

Douglas Marshall and Appletree Press; to Martyn Turner for the foreword and the other words before it; to other researchers in the field, especially L. Perry Curtis; to Dermot Roche, Seamus Dunn and Felicity Hepburn who acted as sounding boards; and to my family for tolerating my obsession.
   The main thanks, however, go to the cartoonists.

The Wild Irish:

Historical Images

1

There were very few peoples in the world who had been presented with the unique privilege of giving up their own nationality and becoming English; but, instead of being eternally grateful, the Irish, who were a most unstable people, had done nothing but create trouble ever since.

Frank Huggett

THE willingness to generalise about racial or national enemies is as old as war and conquest, and the English stereotype of Irishmen may be dated from the twelfth century, with Giraldus Cambrensis' *History of the Conquest of Ireland*, commissioned by Henry II to validate his conquest of the island. Cambrensis provided the first in a long line of comparisons between the inhabitants of Britain and those of Ireland. Britain, he pointed out, was unequalled for its many 'profitable lawes, direction, rules, examples and discourses', while the wild Irish lived in a country 'barren of good things' and continually given up to 'bloud, murther and loathsome outrages' (see Holinshed 1577). Among these outrages were eating human flesh, robbery, sodomy, incest, superstition, and paganism. Nevertheless, the Irish also found time to prevent Henry's effective conquest of their island, and few later examples may be found of such stereotyping until the resurgence of colonial ambition during the sixteenth century.

During the Tudor period, when the English conquest of the island was completed, it began to resume some familiar and novel forms. The English literature of the period generally stresses two characteristics of the Irish, their ignorance and their violence, either of them a convenient justification for a renewal of the conquest. After all, the British monarch had claimed the Irish throne since Henry II's reign, and the prevalence of heresy, treason and disorder was unacceptable—at least until the means of their removal were at hand. The descriptions of the Irish as recalcitrant barbarians in print is not paralleled in the woodcuts and paintings of the time. The defeated Irish, although more rudily dressed than their conquerors, are not distinguishable from them in facial or physical characteristics, and there are few examples of brutal or evil caricature. Indeed the faces have the noble bearing of an honourable foe. In an age which lacked mass media, it may have been important to encourage adverse views of the Irish only among the literate population. At any rate, there appears to have been no fixed stereotype of the Irish among the Elizabethan illiterates, or at least no attempt to create a pictorial one.

During the period of colonisation which followed the conquest the image presented of the Catholic Irish became more hostile and, later, openly

Begorrah and Blood

'The lewder Irish, both clerks and laymen, are sensual and loose above measure', Edmund Campion pointed out in 1571. Nevertheless, measurements of the encyclopedic depth of Irish depravity subsequently became a favourite preoccupation of some of his English fellow countrymen. Stupidity, aggression and superstition were the recurring themes in pamphlets and books about the Irish for the following three centuries. Drawings and cartoons, perhaps for lack of art, were less uncompromising. Even in the drawings of the atrocities during the 1641 rising, the brutal activities of the rebels are not reflected in their faces. Like their victims, they were drawn in the flat and unemotional style of the day.

antagonistic. The 1641 rebellion, the Cromwellian campaigns and the war between James II and William III were all carried out to a background of anti-Irish feeling in England. The murder of Protestants during the 1641 rebellion in particular was described in gory detail both in pamphlets and broadsheets, often accompanied by illustrations, which held a powerful propagandist effect for a long time. Indeed the model established during this period continued until the end of the eighteenth century, when a short-lived liberal orthodoxy reigned, and when representations of the Irish became more complex.

Why did this simple and crude stereotype last so long? Richard Ned

PUNCH, OR THE LONDON CHARIVARI.—MARCH 3, 1866.

Punch

THE FENIAN-PEST.

HIBERNIA. "O MY DEAR SISTER, WHAT *ARE* WE TO DO WITH THESE TROUBLESOME PEOPLE?"
BRITANNIA. "TRY ISOLATION FIRST, MY DEAR, AND THEN——"

Illustrated London News

Punch

THE ENGLISH LABOURER'S BURDEN;
OR, THE IRISH OLD MAN OF THE MOUNTAIN.

[*See Sinbad the Sailor.*]

By the 1860s the image had changed dramatically, and *Punch*'s cartoons about Ireland had been invaded by a caste of simianised Fenians. The Irish famine of the 1840s, before this new image had become fixed, is almost a case study of an ethnic image in the process of changing. The *Illustrated London News* was compassionate towards the awful suffering. *Punch* even accepted that Britain had a moral obligation to provide assistance, but at the same time blamed the Irish for imposing burdens on the long-suffering British taxpayers by their own incompetence: 'It has long been felt that the Irish people are unable to take care of themselves. Everyone has perceived that there must be something wrong about a nation which allows one of

Lebow suggests that it is a feature of all colonial relationships, and that the characteristics attributed to natives by colonisers all over the world—indolence, cowardliness, rashness, violence, brutality—are remarkably uniform. The reason, he argued, lay in the colonists' need to establish their privileges by debasing the conquered. Further, he suggests that the native inhabitants as well as their masters are often persuaded that the stereotype accurately reflects their character and their inferiority, and accept their assigned role. 'By the nineteenth century', Lebow claimed, 'the major characteristics attributed to the Irish—indolence, superstition, dishonesty and a propensity of violence—had remained prominent in the British image for over six

IRISH IBERIAN.   ANGLO-TEUTONIC.   NEGRO.

The Iberians are believed to have been originally an African race, who thousands of years ago spread themselves through Spain over Western Europe. Their remains are found in the barrows, or burying places, in sundry parts of these countries. The skulls are of low, prognathous type. They came to Ireland, and mixed with the natives of the South and West, who themselves are supposed to have been of low type and descendants of savages of the Stone Age, who, in consequence of isolation from the rest of the world, had never been out-competed in the healthy struggle of life, and thus made way, according to the laws of nature, for superior races.

Harper's Weekly

TWO FORCES.

Tenniel/Punch

the finest countries in the world to run to ruin.' The general view that the fault lay in inherent inferiority is well demonstrated by John Constable's 1898 illustrations of racial types.

The main ingredients of the increasingly hostile attitude to Ireland were encapsulated in Sir John Tenniel's 'Two forces', which appeared in *Punch* in 1881. The ape-like image of anarchy was contrasted with the weeping ineffectual Hibernia. Ireland's reality confronted her potential. Only Britannia's protection stood between order and chaos. These themes of violence, ineffectuality and British benevolence dominated English cartoons about Ireland during the second

half of the nineteenth century—a tendency which aroused considerable resentment among Irish cartoonists.

hundred years. There can be no doubt that by then the Irish displayed many of these characteristics to a greater extent than did their English neighbours' (Lebow 1976, 78).

Lebow's analysis fails to distinguish sufficiently between the different attitudes towards the native Irish held by the mainland British and those who came to settle the conquered lands, especially in Ulster. Following the military conquest Britain's interest in Ireland was limited to ensuring that Ireland did not become a commercial rival nor a factor in British internal political disputes. Outside these two main concerns the control of the island was left to the settlers, who were allowed all the paraphernalia of independ-

Matt Morgan/*Punch*

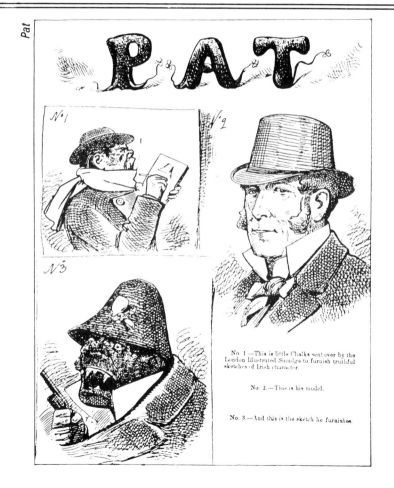

Pat

Alongside them ran another more tolerant category of cartoons. These were 'Irish Bulls', cartoons where the joke lay in pointing out a rather endearing contrariness in the Irish character. These precursors of the music-hall Irish joke appeared regularly in *Punch* for a century or more from the 1850s. They shared one important quality with the simian

ence, including their own parliament, church and judiciary. So the problem of dealing with the indigenous population passed from the mother country to the colonists, and into the hands of those who were most aware of the threat hanging over them. To this small minority, who monopolised political, administrative, social and economic power, it was essential to maintain and emphasise the distinctions between themselves and the more numerous and potentially rebellious native population. Assimilation was not only un-characteristic of the period; it also represented the threat of inundation. Dominance and distance were the order of the seventeenth and eighteenth centuries, and encouraged the maintenance of hostile attitudes towards the

Phil May/Punch

Mrs. O'Brady: "SHURE I WANT TO BANK TWENTY POUNDS. CAN I DRAW IT OUT QUICK IF I WANT IT?"
Postmaster: "INDADE, MRS. O'BRADY, YOU CAN DRAW IT OUT TOMORROW IF YOU GIVE ME A WAKE'S NOTICE!"

Punch

Harper's Weekly

24 *"The Ignorant Vote: Honors Are Easy."* Nast depicts the balance of political forces in America during Reconstruction with this cartoon of emancipated slaves in the south, carrying as much weight as the nasty, brutish, and simian Irish-American voter in the north. The proverbial clay pipe in his hatband reinforces the "White's" ethnicity. (*Harper's Weekly*, 9 December 1876.)

cartoons. The benign condescension of the former joined with the racial stereotyping of the latter to confirm Mr Punch's frequently expressed view that 'the Irish are clearly incapable of managing their own affairs'.

Tourist (at Irish hotel). "YOU SEEM TIRED, PAT!"
Waiter. "YISS, SORR. UP VERY EARLY THIS MORNING—HALF-PAST SIX!"
Tourist. "I DON'T CALL HALF-PAST SIX EARLY!"
Waiter (quickly). "WELL, HALF-PAST FIVE, THIN!"

It is worth noting that the apelike image of the Irishman crossed the Atlantic, and

was featured in a number of cartoons by Thomas Nast in *Harper's Weekly*. The emergence of Ulster as a complicating element in British politics was regarded

Irish.

So the main generators of the anti-Irish views were the planters, and the stereotype began to assume the character of civil conflict rather than war, with an accompanying increase in bitterness. No doubt this hostile stereotype was also generally accepted in Britain, but disapproval became explicit on the mainland only during those periods of political dispute when Ireland became a sub-plot to British constitutional disputes. The most antagonistic Irish images were concentrated in those periods when the internal threat to Protestant control in Ireland coincided with an external threat to the stability of institutions in Britain. The 1641 rebellion during the English Civil War,

THE SLEEPLESS BEAUTY.

Mr. Asquith (*the Fairy Prince*). "I DON'T SO MUCH MIND ALL THIS BRIAR STUFF; IT'S THE LADY AT THE END THAT MAKES ME NERVOUS."

Bernard Partridge/*Punch*

STARTING THE SETTLEMENT.

L. Raven Hill/*Punch*

NEWSPAPER REPORTER "And now, ur, your epitaph?"
SHADE OF ROBERT EMMET "NOT YET!"

Arthur Booth/*Dublin Opinion*

with apprehension by cartoonists. The Irish were trouble enough, it seemed, without this further complexity. British cartoonists dutifully applauded her loyalty, but distrusted the fierceness with which it was expressed. As a result, the female figure who came to represent the province, in contrast to the mute and helpless Hibernia, had a distinctly shrewish aspect.

The ending of the Anglo–Irish war, and the partitioning of the island, were greeted with universal relief in Britain. Northern Ireland began her existence with hearty good wishes. She was then forgotten. Between 1922 and 1942 there was a grand total of fifteen Irish cartoons in *Punch*, and only three of them referred to Northern Ireland. South of the border, too, the warning in the first issue of *Dublin Opinion* that the struggle for independence remained uncompleted was not repeated in later issues.

the war between James II and William III and the 1798 rebellion with its threat of French support were such periods, when printer and illustrator combined to present images of uncontrolled Irish barbarity and violence.

The Victorians

A systematic study of these earlier images has yet to be carried out, for academic interest in English images of Ireland may be claimed to originate only in the first half of the nineteenth century. The reasons are not hard to find. As long as British interests were preserved through its surrogates in Dublin Castle, British interest in Ireland was relatively low-key and relatively benign. The books written by such eighteenth and early nineteenth century English travellers as Young, Twiss and Barrow occasionally betray disapproval of Irish habits, particularly religious and hygenic, but were not unsympathetic to the condition of Irish peasants. Even into the mid-nineteenth century, as Mansergh has demonstrated, English-based authors such as Marx, Mills, Nassau Senior and Ricardo were inclined to attribute the conditions pertaining there to economic abuse rather than inherent racial inferiority (see Mansergh 1965). In particular the system of land tenure was held accountable for the persistent poverty. Nevertheless, alongside these more serious socio-political analyses, there emerged around the middle of the century a much less favourable stereotype, one which may be related to a coincidence of both political and social changes.

L. Perry Curtis, in his fascinating study *Apes and Angels: The Irishman in Victorian Caricature* (1971), regards this change as reaching its completion during the 1860s and lasting until the First World War. During this period Paddy, the 'feckless, amusing, bibulous and apolitical stage-Irishman or Teague of an earlier epoch, evolved into the distinctly dangerous ape-man of the later-nineteenth century' (Curtis 1971, 4). His appearance was rough and violent and his face had the flaring nostrils, protruding lower lip and receding chin which Victorian cartoonists attributed to apes, gorillas and the races which occupied the lower rungs in the hierarchy of human species. The caricature neatly encapsulated those Irish qualities which were defined in greater depth in the contemporary written media—rashness, instability, indolence, violence and subnormality—and they stood in explicit comparison with the qualities which had made England great. The contrast was neatly summarised as early as 1836 by the young Benjamin Disraeli in *The Times:*

> The Irish hate our free and fertile isle. They hate our order, our civilisation, our enterprising industry, our sustained courage, our decorous liberty, our pure

religion. This wild, reckless, indolent, uncertain and superstitious race has no sympathy with the English character. (*Times*, April 18 1836)

In effect these simian barbarians were the very antithesis of the Athenian attributes with which the Victorian Englishman endowed his own race. Implicit in the image was the patent incompetence of the Irish to deal with the self-government they sought.

Although he acknowledges that hostile images of the Irish—even occasional simian metaphors—may be found before the 1860s, Curtis argues that they lose their variety from that period: 'In the 1860s Paddy began to look like the offspring of a liaison between a gorilla father and a prognathous

Riots and Rioters

Mike Williams/*Punch*

"Hello... Is that the Guinness Book of Records?"

As early as 1841 Mr. Punch observed that the chief delight of the Irish 'seems to consist in getting into all manner of scrapes, for the main purpose of displaying their ingenuity by getting out of them again'. Consequently, while the Civil Rights marches of 1968 and the riots of 1969 took cartoonists and the media in general by surprise, it did not take long to find an appropriate response. Civil rights, it was universally decided, were clearly a good thing, and riots an unavoidable by-product of them. The first reaction was not to attack the disturbances, but to treat them as a humorous novelty. There was even a measure of good-natured stereotyping. After all, the Irish like nothing better than a good brawl.

mother' (Curtis 1971, 37). This particular image, which dominated the British caricatures of the Irish for the rest of the century, resulted from the coincidence of two developments. The great debate on social Darwinism, with its 'gorilla controversy' between Thomas Hardy and Samuel Wilberforce the Bishop of Oxford, encouraged traditionalists to find a relationship between the apes and those whom they most feared or despised. The Fenian dynamiters and bombers of the same period seemed to confirm the media's already hostile view of Ireland, and emphasised the mindless violence which had been noted earlier. 'Just as Darwinism appeared to lay bare the ugly realities of the struggle for survival, so Fenianism appeared to reveal the

Doll/*Irish Independent*

Rowel Friers/*Fortnight*

We shall overcome

It was not long before the first expressions of concern. By 1969 sectarian riots were dominating the news, and were more difficult to regard frivolously. Rowel Friers' concern about growing disregard for legal processes was illustrated by marching feet trampling over lawyers; but the feet belong to respectable citizens, not hooligans—indeed, the cartoon could also be interpreted as a comment on the law's delay. More prescient, or alarmist, was

elemental beast in Irish character' (Curtis 1971, 102). All that was required to fix the image firmly was its vivid expression by Tenniel, Morgan, Bowcher and other gifted caricaturists in *Punch, The Tomahawk* and the popular comic weeklies which emerged around the middle of the century. The result was the emergence of a strong, and widely accepted, image of an Irish race clearly unqualified for the serious business of government, and entirely unfit for the Home Rule which they were seeking.

An interesting aspect of Curtis' thesis was the reaction to this apelike parody in the United States and in Ireland itself. In America the arrival of large numbers of Irish immigrants to the urban centres of the east coast

"*You called, sorr?*"

EM/Punch

Colin Wheeler/New Statesman

Calman/Sunday Times

McLachlan's warning that the I.R.A. could be rekindled from the petrol bombs of rioters. Inevitably the gunman's face was a throwback to the previous century's imagery.

The arrival of the army in August 1969 simplified matters for most British cartoonists, and the media in general rallied behind the flag. Grievances may remain, was the message, but surely the time had arrived to call off the violence? Leave it to the law and the army. Cartoonists often adopted the device of presenting soldiers as neutral and innocent commentators on an increasingly complex and irritating conflict. Their role was that of innocents between two groups of fanatics.

during the post-Famine years produced an antipathy markedly similar to that in Britain. This was reflected in a tendency for American cartoonists to depict Irishmen as apes in a manner similar to that in Britain. Thomas Nast, the famous nineteenth century American cartoonist, established the model of what Curtis described as 'Irish–American apes', and many others followed. One Nast cartoon, 'St Patrick's Day 1867: The Day We Celebrate' (*Harper's Weekly*, December 9 1867), was a picture of brutish, rioting Irishmen attacking the police, and was framed between the words Rum and Blood. Another entitled 'The Ignorant Vote: Honors are Easy' (*Harper's Weekly*, December 9 1876) represented an evenly balanced set of scales: on the southern side sat

Gerald Scarfe/*Sunday Times*

The forms of Northern Ireland's violence altered greatly after the growth of I.R.A. violence during 1970, and the loyalist reaction to it. Riots were more infrequent and, when they became the subject of cartoons, their treatment was increasingly general. The expressions of abhorrence by Scarfe and Friers were really comments on the apparent intractability of the problem. Apparently there was little more to say.

Rowel Friers/*Riotous Living*

a grinning emancipated black slave; on the northern an apelike Paddy, identified by the traditional badge of the clay pipe in his hat.

Nevertheless there were differences in emphasis between the British and American images of the Irish. Whereas in Britain the main characteristic was violence and the main target the Fenians, in the United States Paddy more frequently represented gullibility and corruption, and the targets were the Irish–American politicians who used this to their advantage.

Not surprisingly, cartoonists in Ireland took a different view. Here the images were partially reversed. In these cartoons, as Curtis put it, 'the forces of good represented by Erin, Pat and the Parnellites, were confronting the forces of evil represented by Dublin Castle, the apparatus of coercion, evicting landlords, Orangemen, and fair-weather patriots' (Curtis 1971, 76). Although the English were rarely simianised in Dublin weeklies, the Irish themselves were often drawn as angels. Pat, usually represented as a well-to-do tenant farmer rather than a peasant, was a pleasant, handsome chap, with square chin and honest eyes. These images were deliberate reactions to the hostile images of the Irish in British cartoons, as was frequently illustrated by the cartoons of O'Hea and Orphen in *Pat* and *The Jarvey* showing a bemused Irishman confronting the image drawn of him by English cartoonists. Most important, they demonstrate both an awareness and a resentment about the work of British cartoonists, which challenges Ned Lebow's argument that the hostile images, by a self-fulfilling process, had persuaded the Irish that they were based on reality.

Lebow believes that Curtis has exaggerated the importance of the simianisation process. Anti-Irish feeling in Britain can be found since the twelfth century, he points out, and was only altered to reflect the fashions and concerns of particular periods. 'The only novelty in Victorian times was the fact that the prejudice was increasingly articulated in the terminology of racial differentiation. Racist expressions were merely the age-old Irish prejudice couched in the jargon of the day.' Lebow goes on to suggest that 'an argument can be made that anti-Irish sentiment in Britain actually declined in the second half of the nineteenth century' (Lebow 1976, 15). Lebow's study is focussed on the 1840s when Daniel O'Connell's repeal movement was exciting considerable concern in Britain, and he argues that the antipathy to Ireland in *The Times*, *Punch* and other leading publications were at least as bitter as those of the 1860s. There were three schools of thought with respect to Irish problems, according to Lebow: the repeal thesis, the view of a radical minority who favoured repeal of the act of Union; the Liberal thesis, which, while advocating reform, argued that the fundamental problem was the Irish character; and the Orange thesis, which saw the issue as essentially one of law and order. The last two dominated public opinion and official policy during the century.

The Three Faces of Ireland

In fact, as both Curtis and Lebow acknowledge, the English image of the Irish during the nineteenth century was highly ambivalent. Certainly a major theme was the unstable, violent Paddy, predictable only in his periodic attraction to violence for its own sake; as H. S. Constable put it, 'one sign of

Political Personalities

Lacking detailed knowledge of Northern Ireland, one of the first responses of some cartoonists was to focus on the new characters thrown up by the conflict. Easily the most popular of these were Bernadette Devlin and Ian Paisley.

David Langdon/*Punch*

"It'll look a bit strange in 'Hansard'—'The Hon. Member for Mid Ulster, bracket, long low wolf whistles, bracket.'"

lowness of type, or barbarism, in the West Irish is their indifference about human life. This is the case with most barbarous people' (Constable 1898, 62). There was another image, however, which also attracted British cartoonists throughout the nineteenth and early twentieth centuries. This presented Paddy as a childlike, feckless, contradictory peasant, stupid but lovable, and addicted to the contrariness which so delighted Victorian tourists and still appeals to music-hall and television comedians. Thus, when an angler in *Punch* asked a peasant who was digging up the floor of his cottage, 'Hullo, Pat, what are you about now?' Pat replied, 'Shure, I'm raising the roof a bit, yer Honour–r.' A tourist seeking directions in 1873 was informed, 'If I was

Jim Fitzpatrick/*Hibernia*

BERNADETTE DEVLIN

Heath/*Spectator*

The apotheosis of Bernadette.

going there I wouldn't start from here.' In these examples of what were called 'Irish bulls' the relationship between the English tourist and Pat—a more indulgent form of address than Paddy—was that of a governess and a mentally retarded child. Affection and kindness were predominant, tinged by exasperation. The bulls emphasised equally Pat's charm and his inability to cope with life's demands. In these images the characteristic Irish trait was an obsequious and naive cunning, but not violence. Pat, unlike Paddy, would never have used a blunderbuss or a bomb. He was the victim of circumstances rather than an aggressor. In both stereotypes, however, he was obviously capricious and incompetent, and the Victorians were no more dis-

The caricatures of Bernadette Devlin were particularly instructive. In 1969 and 1970 she captivated the press as an epitome of the Sixties— youthful, confident, irreverent and miniskirted. Langdon and other British and Irish cartoonists were equally enthusiastic and reverential. Heath in the *Spectator* was rather more cynical, and other cartoonists became uneasy when she began to offend the stereotype they had given her. Her involvement in violence in Derry and subsequent imprisonment led to a sharp decline in her popularity as a subject. Dobson coped with the new complication by suggesting a split personality, while

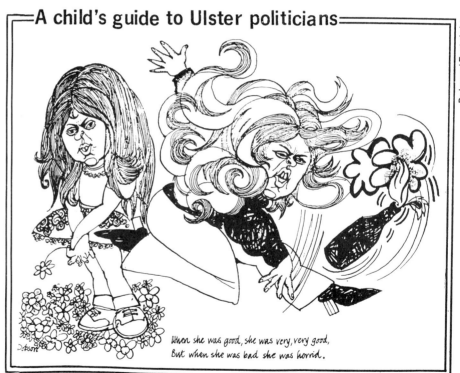

A child's guide to Ulster politicians

Dobson/*Fortnight*

When she was good, she was very, very good,
But when she was bad she was horrid.

posed to entrust responsibility to Lear's Fool than to a Celtic Caliban.

This mixture of irritation and avuncular concern was well illustrated by the treatment of the Irish famine of the 1840s in British newspapers and magazines. R. G. Price, writing in 1971, claimed that '*Punch* took the radical view that starvation and poverty were the same whether in the rookeries of Whitechapel or the crumbling cottages of Galway' (Price 1971).

The truth is less flattering. It is true that the *Illustrated London News*, *Punch* and even *The Times* all had a generalised sympathy for the condition of the suffering Irish, and accepted some moral obligation of fraternal charity. In John Leech's cartoon, for instance, Brittania and Caledonia were

Rowel Friers/*Riotous Living*

Friers identified three Bernadettes. By 1978 Littleman's cartoon in *Hibernia* showed how much of the early lustre had disappeared. But the entire cycle illustrates the speed at which stereotypes can be established, and how difficult it is to alter an image once it has been set.

Littleman/*Hibernia*

reprimanded for insufficient sympathy with the Irish Cinderella (*Punch* 1846, 181). The drawings in the *Illustrated London News* also expressed compassion. However this general commiseration was surpassed by fury that the means of its remedy had to come from the pockets of English tax-payers. 'What is an Englishman made for but to work?' asked *The Times*. 'What is an Irishman made for but to sit at his cabin door, read O'Connell's speeches and abuse the English?' (*The Times*, January 26 1847). Indeed the same paper managed to find benefits in the famine:

> For our own part we regard the potato blight as a blessing. When the Celts once

Doll/Irish Press

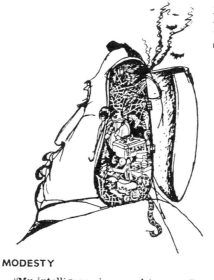

Fortnight

MODESTY

"My intelligence is second to none."
Newsletter 6·7-70.

Ged/Irish Times

COULD MUHAMMAD PUT HIM OUT iN THE 13TH?

The main problem posed for cartoonists by Ian Paisley was whether to emphasise his venom or his absurdity. He was a popular butt for cartoonists on both sides of the Irish border, the treatment was universally hostile, and he was often taken to represent the mainstream Protestant position, as in Cogan's cartoon which contrasts Paisley and his malevolent supporters with a shining Bernadette Devlin surrounded by happy, honest faces. What effect this may have had on public perceptions of the Unionist position raises an interesting question.

cease to be potatophagi, they must become carniverous. With the taste of meats will grow an appetite for them; with the appetite, the readiness to earn them. (*The Times*, September 22 1846).

What particularly rankled was the perceived failure of the Irish to show proper servitude or gratitude for English largesse. When parliament at last voted £50,000 for famine relief in 1849, *Punch*'s annoyance was excited by a simultaneous call by the bishop of Tuam for an Irish papal levy: 'We are to give Ireland, who cannot feed herself, but can subsidise the Pope, £50,000 and more' (*Punch* 1849, 82). The suspicion that the Irish were accepting

J. Cogan/*Hibernia*

"Change lieders and we'll fight you all over again."

English charity while buying guns for rebellion aroused equal rage from cartoonists (*Punch* 1846, 245).

The balancing act between benign and hostile views is as evident in *Punch*'s text as in its cartoons. Witness extracts from two separate lists of the 'Fallacies of the Irish' in 1848, their heavy sarcasm occasionally interrupted by benevolence:

> That the English like lending—or rather giving—them money, and being abused for it afterwards.
>
> That they have a right to be idle, and that England has a right to support them in their idleness.

Richard Willson/*Spectator*

William Whitelaw and Enoch Powell were also popular subjects for caricature, but their contact with Northern Ireland did not enhance either image. Willson's premature confidence in Whitelaw's ability to sort out the problem, for example, reflected British confidence in his ability, but did not protect him when he failed to deliver the goods.

The pattern of these caricatures provides a sombre lesson. Those who were identified as villains at the start, like Paisley, became deeper villains as the conflict developed. But those who were presumptuous enough to deceive the cartoonists that they represented hope, like Devlin and Whitelaw, were soon abandoned by their own image-makers. It was a game no one could win.

It is not necessary to discharge a gun to discharge a debt.
That the English are at all opposed to them, and not anxious to assist them.
(*Punch* 1848, 1–5, 214)

Alongside the images of violence and incompetence which so dominated English Victorian opinion of Ireland is a third, perhaps underrated, metaphor. This is the figure of Hibernia or Rosaleen or Erin—a popular device of cartoonists in the period before the First World War. She was a young, beautiful and chaste maiden, much given to tears and vapours about the state of Ireland. Her essential qualities were helplessness, good intentions and inability to cope, and her role was that of John Bull's niece, and the younger frail sister of a strapping Britannia. She was the third face of the Irish character, and appeared as a contrast to the simian brutal bomber in Tenniel's most noted Irish cartoon (*Punch*, October 29 1881). While brutal Paddy and incompetent Pat represented the reality of nineteenth century Ireland, Hibernia stood for its future potential. Her qualities, it was hoped, were submerged, only needing the encouragement and protection of her Britannic sister to be realised. Until the happy day when, presumably, Hibernia matured into a less formidable form of Britannia, she needed support and direction. So this third image of Ireland, like the other two, was also one which emphasised Ireland's incapacity to run its own affairs. If self-government could not be entrusted to either the Celtic Caliban or Lear's fool, neither could it be handed over to Ophelia.

Home Rule and Ulster

With the growing agitation for Home Rule from the 1880s, and its subsequent adoption by Gladstone and the Liberals, the English images of Ireland underwent a gradual but discernable change. The transfer of the struggle from the streets to the Houses of Parliament was greeted with approval, and the prevalent view of cartoonists changed from antagonism to an amused condescension. John Redmond, who led the Irish Parliamentary Party in the years preceding and during the First World War, became the personification of the prospective Dublin parliament. Surrounded by pigs and bedecked in shamrock-embroidered waistcoat, battered hat with clay pipe attached, and knee-breeches, with a shillelagh sticking out from the hip pocket, he was ridiculed as the potential Irish leader. A comic leprechaun sat on a throne as 'Redmondus Rex' or as the centrepiece of an imagined Irish postage stamp (*Punch*, May 1 1912). No elaboration was needed. The theme was clear. While there was no longer strong antagonism to the prospect of Home Rule, the idea had become an occasion for humour.

More difficult for cartoonists was the problem of loyalist opposition to Home Rule. Within Ireland itself, the theme became more popular during the 1880s in magazines like *Nomad's Weekly* and *Blarney*. However the question of Ulster hardly featured at all in English drawings about Ireland until the 1880s, except when its relative prosperity was contrasted with the other parts of the island. Some more astute observers saw potential trouble. 'L'Ulster est L'Ecosse de l'Irlande' wrote de Beaumont in 1839, and *Punch* made passing reference to the Irish Orange flower as early as 1847. It was only from the 1880s however that Ulster's opposition to Home Rule heralded the arrival of a new actor on the stage. Even then, Mansergh pointed out, the question of Ulster itself was generally regarded as quite insignificant: 'The cause was greater than Ulster or than Ireland. It was the cause of Empire. And it was that which gave to the Ulster and to the Irish Question its critical significance in the history of British imperialism'. (Mansergh 1965, 192).

Despite this, no consensus on Ulster emerged in the cartoons of *Punch*, but rather a mixture of apprehension and amusement. Storm clouds and pious hopes abound, and the importance of restraint is repeatedly stressed. The Ulstermen drilling with wooden rifles and without uniforms were drawn as toy soldiers, and Mr Punch sternly admonished their leader Carson, more in sorrow than in anger: 'So Ulster will fight, Mr Carson. Then Ulster will be wrong' (*Punch*, January 24 1912). In another cartoon, Asquith was portrayed as a knight in shining armour, about to hack through the briars imprisoning the maiden Ulster, his enthusiasm somewhat dampened by apprehension of the virago he will be releasing. There was a sense of relief in 1914 among politicians and cartoonists alike that the war at least provided an agreed approach to the issue—one which stressed the need for unity in the face of adversity and the fact that all were in this together. By and large, the media did not react with enthusiasm to the emergence of the Ulster issue, and many accepted partition as the best of a collection of unpalatable alternatives.

As a result the fifty years following partition stand in striking contrast to the half century before it. In effect the popularity of Ireland as a cartoon theme disappeared almost overnight. Between 1922 and 1942 *Punch* printed a total of only fifteen cartoons about Ireland, and only three of these were about Northern Ireland. Even in Ireland, a selection of the best cartoons from Ireland's most·popular magazine of the post-partition years had only one cartoon on partition, and that was in the very first issue in 1922 (*Fifteen Years of Dublin Opinion*, 1937).

This decline was the result of a variety of factors: in Britain the relationship between hostile stereotyping of the Irish and direct British involvement in Irish affairs, which has been demonstrated in earlier periods, may also explain the loss of interest in Ireland after partition; responsibility for the island had been transferred to the Free State in the south and to the surrogate Unionist government in the north, so that the new unthreatening Irish could again be depicted as the likable Paddies of the earlier Irish bulls. In the United States, for the most part, the issue of partition lacked the clarity and appeal of the struggle for Irish independence. Nearer home the lack of cartoons on Northern Ireland may be as related to the shortage of outlets for cartoonists as to a decline of interest in partition. In all cases, given the media's general apathy about Northern Ireland, many cartoonists may have been forgiven for assuming that, apart from localised grievances, the Irish question had at last been resolved.

The riots of 1969 were to change their minds.

Riot or War?

The Dilemma for British Cartoonists

2

The Press is not an independent institution. There is no free Press. It is locked into the structure of society.

Eamonn McCann

'NO longer offensive, no longer apologetic, *Punch* enters the seventies at ease with its neighbouring isle.' This at any rate was the view of R.G.G Price about the magazine's relationship with Ireland, expressed in a hearty and eulogistic article published in *Punch* on January 6, 1971. Six months earlier Mahood, the *Punch* cartoonist most interested in Northern Ireland, had featured a twelve-cartoon collection entitled 'The Bigotry Cup', which suggested a more uneasy association: 'Play can begin at any time, but usually starts after the pubs close. A petrol bomb is tossed to decide who retaliates first'. A Religious Supplies shop, displaying in its window Holy Petrol, Blessed Shillelahs (sic) and Sharp-edged Bibles, is accompanied by the instruction, 'Anything can be worn that is a danger to opponents. Boots should be well-studded with protruding nails. Plaster casts on broken limbs can be inset with broken glass' (*Punch*, July 8 1970). Far from adopting a benevolent view towards Northern Ireland, *Punch* and much of the rest of the British media viewed its conflict through an increasingly jaundiced eye.

At first sight the British press, and its cartoonists, followed a complete cycle in their treatment of Northern Ireland between 1968 and 1981. The changing approaches of cartoonists corresponded closely to phases in the conflict itself, and were essentially related to the level of direct British involvement in the government of Northern Ireland. Before the Civil Rights march to Dungannon in August 1968 there was little sign of either knowledge or interest in the province's affairs; this might be termed the Phase of ignorance. The twelve months from August 1968, culminating in the arrival of the British army in Northern Ireland, were marked by surprise that such dramatic events could take place in one's back yard; the generally simplistic reactions to this constitute the Phase of naïveté. The Phase of exasperation, with its abortive attempts to reach political settlement, ended with the abolition of the Northern Ireland parliament and the introduction of Direct Rule in March 1972. The next phase saw the worst of the violence, the failure of the power-sharing experiment in May 1974, and a growing revulsion for Northern Ireland and all that went on there. The cycle was completed by a final Phase of apathy, which still persists in 1983. The repetitiveness and resilience of violence eventually diminished the attraction of the theme, which was only spasmodically revived by extraordinary developments in the conflict, like the 1979 Papal visit or the hunger strikes of 1980 and 1981. This pattern is reflected in the quantity of cartoons produced on the theme. In all the publications under study, only one cartoon relating to Northern Ireland appeared in 1968; having reached a peak of almost 200 in 1972, by 1978 there were only twelve. These variations in the attraction of Northern Ireland to cartoonists were largely determined by the extent to which it affected internal British concerns.

Naïveté replaces Ignorance: August 1968-August 1969

Cartoonists in Britain, having almost completely ignored Northern Ireland during the 1960s, were unprepared for the first Civil Rights march in Dungannon on August 26 1968. The announcement of a second march in Derry on October 5, and the prospect of violence accompanying it, led to a five-fold increase of British press coverage (Davies 1970) and an influx of bemused and confused reporters. Eamonn McCann caught the atmosphere well:

> Immediately after 5 October 1968 dozens of journalists descended on Northern Ireland. At one point the *Mirror* had twelve people in Derry. Some, mindful of the May days in France that year, spent much of their time trying to identify a local Danny the Red. Others would wander into the Bogside and ask if they could be introduced to someone who had been discriminated against. (McCann 1971)

The problem was even greater for cartoonists than for reporters. They did not have the time to explore the complexities of the issue, and were clearly anxious about plunging into waters which might prove deeper and more dangerous than they appeared. So, virtually without exception, British cartoonists confined their attention to the shallows.

In particular they concentrated on the new personalities who had come to the fore during the early Troubles. Ian Paisley was a godsend, in the cartooning rather than the theological sense. Not only did he represent a style and stance that seemed eccentric and extravagant to British readers, but he served as a convenient metaphor for loyalist bigotry and intransigence. *Punch* portrayed him as a living reminder of our primeval origins (December 18 1968), and Heath in the *Spectator* captioned his besashed, ranting figure with 'Who said music-hall was dead?' (*Spectator* February 28 1969) At this stage there was a tendency to regard Paisley as a preposterous anachronism, sufficiently bizarre as to be amusing. As the conflict developed, however, Paisley was seen less as a burlesque bigot and more as a dangerous demagogue. In this he was taken to represent the views of the entire unionist community. Even during their initial cautious sallies into the complexities of the Ulster question, British cartoonists had no hesitation in casting the entire

The Paraphernalia of War

Twelve years of conflict has produced a remarkable and controversial supply of terrorist and anti-terrorist paraphernalia. Black hoods and sensory deprivation, armalite rifles, rubber and plastic bullets, CS gas—all exercised a fascination for cartoonists, especially soldier-cartoonists. Sawn-off shotguns and silencers were the sort of ambiguous terms which encouraged cartoonists to provide pictorial versions of the Irish jokes which had become so popular during the 1970s.

Dredge/Private Eye

"There'll be no cock-ups this time, Boss—Paddy's bringing in some sawn-off shotguns!"

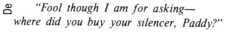

De la Nongerede/Punch

"Fool though I am for asking—where did you buy your silencer, Paddy?"

I SAY, JOLLY GOOD OF YOU CHAPS TO COME!

BRITISH INVITE IRA TO TALKS

BLAH BLAH BLAH YOUR DEMANDS BLAH   BLAHBLAH NO MORE BLOODY BOMBINGS BLAH   BLAH BLAH TROOP WITHDRAWALS BLAH BLAH   BLAH BLAH BLAH FREE BLAH BLAH GOV'T BLAH BLAH

SEEMED LIKE NICE BLOKES, REALLY...   RIGHTO.. OH, THEY'VE FORGOTTEN THEIR BRIEFCA...

Republican News

Protestant community in the villain's role. Later their attitude towards the Catholic minority also changed, but never to the extent where there was much sympathy for unionist apprehensions.

If Paisley was the epitome of evil for the cartoonists, Bernadette Devlin stood for virtue. Her passion, youth and dress seemed to embody the swinging sixties, and captivated the press. 'She's Bernadette, she's 21, she's an MP and she's swinging', rhapsodised the *Express.* 'The girl whose honesty, vision and courage has made her the most talked of person in Irish politics for a long time' (April 11 1969). The *Sketch* was also won over: 'She is an orphan, has big grey eyes, a Terry Thomas gap in her teeth, wears faded blue jeans

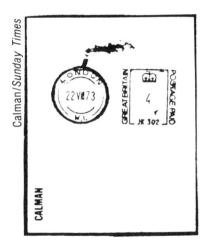

Calman/Sunday Times

Trog/Observer

ITS NOT TROOPS THEY NEED ITS MISSIONARIES

Wheeler/New Statesman

'THIS IS A POLICE RECORDING. THANK YOU FOR YOUR BOMB HOAX CALL. YOUR NEAREST PSYCHIATRIC HOSPITAL IS AT..

Bombs were more difficult to treat frivolously, but too tempting to ignore completely. The result was a succession of parcel bombs, letter bombs, bombs thrown from helicopters or left in briefcases, self-destructive bombers and bomb-disposing robots. The treatment was largely determined by the location of the bomb: humour was only possible when the bomb had exploded in an unidentifiable target; Northern Irish bombs rarely featured at all; but the response was bitter when IRA bombs were planted in Britain, and the bombers were often represented as subhuman psychopaths. In such cases the only humour took the form of Wheeler's sardonic comments on the bomber and their victims.

and would get lost in a crowd of three' (April 22 1969). Cartoonists were not slow to follow. Giles showed middle-aged MPs dressing up for the House of Commons after her election to parliament (*Sunday Express*, April 20 1969), and Langdon had MPs speculating about how her arrival would be reported in Hansard: 'The Hon. Members for Mid-Ulster, bracket, long low wolf whistles, bracket' (*Punch*, April 30 1969). The honeymoon was shortlived. Her involvement in the Bogside riots in 1969, and what was seen as her open contempt for parliament, produced an abrupt volte-face. 'Whatever happened to Bernadette?' asked Marjorie Proops in the *Mirror* (July 8 1969), a question exactly reproduced in the *Mail* (August 18 1969). For many cartoonists her transformation from Joan of Arc to a Catholic version of Paisley was difficult to manage, and her popularity as a subject simply faded away. Her failure to conform to the image which they had awarded her was explained by a change on her part; the possibility that it may have been encouraged by their own adoption of the wrong cliché was not considered.

The Growth of Exasperation: August 1969-March 1972

Every attempt to isolate historical phases is subject to dispute, but August 1969 certainly marked a significant turning point in Northern Ireland's conflict. The sectarian rioting which had been building up during the summer reached its climax, and the British army was introduced to the streets of Belfast and Londonderry. This in turn initiated thirty months of the most dramatic violence and change: during this period four new political parties were established in the province, the Provisional IRA was formed and began its campaign of violence, the loyalist UDA went on to the streets, Internment was introduced and ultimately, in March 1972, Northern Ireland's government and parliament were replaced by Direct Rule from Westminster. These developments were sufficiently dynamic to keep the interest of most British cartoonists. More significant, they altered fundamentally the way in which they regarded the conflict.

It was the arrival of the army rather than the riots which they had been directed to quell that brought about the change. The riots themselves were regarded with relative good nature by the cartoonists—largely an extension of the Irish love for a good fight. As one of Mahood's soldiers pointed out to his mate, 'if God had wanted the Irish to be happy, He wouldn't have allowed St Patrick to introduce religion in the first place' (*Punch*, August 18 1971). Soldiers were often used as a Greek chorus, dispassionately commenting on the action. Belsky's squaddies, for example, besieged by rioters, speculate hopefully that Orange parades might be switched to Holland if Britain joined the Common Market (*New Statesman*, July 16 1971). Indeed the great majority of cartoons about the riots adopted this device of viewing them through the eyes of outsiders—soldiers, visiting Englishmen, politicians—who regarded the riots in Belfast and Derry with detachment and a touch of condescension. Heath's two men wondering 'which particular group of the meek are going to inherit Belfast' are clearly talking about a species of humanity beyond the understanding of decent folk (*Spectator*, August 9 1969).

The army itself caused few problems for cartoonists. The early cartoons reflected a general euphoria, as troops were welcomed with tea and sandwiches to the Catholic areas of Belfast. Cheerful Tommies were shown rescuing smiling Mother Macrees from the Belfast floods in August 1970, and the unanimous view was one of compassionate, professional soldiers battling valiantly against impossible odds. When the first criticisms of army behaviour were made, there was an equally unanimous reaction. Allegations of army violence during the Falls road curfew in July 1970 were greeted with anger and disbelief: 'Soldiers who have been jeered, assailed with bricks and bottles and shot at are bound to be under some strain', a *Daily Express* editorial pointed out. 'In fact the Army deserves the highest praise for its patience in face of constant provocation. Those who denigrate the soldiers will find no sympathy whatsoever among the British people' (July 7 1970). Cummings supported this stance with a cartoon showing soldiers knocking politely before searching houses. The theme was echoed by Mac in the *Daily Sketch* (July 7 1970): as soldiers seize a pile of arms from an Irish house, their owner protests, 'There! What did oi tell yez! Looting again'. Sympathy for the soldiers increased as the IRA campaign against the army intensified. The killing of three Scottish soldiers in March 1971 by the recently formed Provisionals produced a powerful and prescient cartoon by Scarfe in the *Sunday Times* (March 14 1971) showing their blood creating the first cracks in a dam, and warning of the deluge to come.

The presence of the British army in Ireland also triggered off a number of conditioned responses among cartoonists in Britain. In particular, the IRA began to feature in cartoons long before, in the view of most responsible commentators, they were a major element in the conflict. Often they were merely an adjunct to other themes; in September 1969, before the Provisionals had even been formed, Heath's IRA gunmen who had kidnapped Harold Wilson were told, in response to a ransom telephone call, that they could keep him (*Spectator*, September 13). In such circumstances there were obvious difficulties in finding a suitably updated image for the IRA. Some cartoonists took the easy way out, and provided them with armbands or hats with 'IRA' helpfully written on them. Cummings identified them by small stature, and a curious mask which covered the upper half of their faces, leaving room underneath for vaguely simian jaws; he was still determinedly using it in 1978.

For most cartoonists, however, it was simply a case of continuing from where the image had been left gathering dust since 1921: in 1969 and 1970 every cartoon IRA man was wrapped in a trench coat. Indeed, Heath still had his IRA man trench-coated in 1972, although by that time the dark glasses

Torture or III-treatment?

SNATCH SQUAD

POVERTY · PRIVILEGE · I.R.A. · BIGOTRY · UNIONIST RIGHT WING

'What are you waiting for? All you have to do is ignore the others and go for the feller in the trench-coat.'

Horner/*New Statesman*

No issues in Northern Ireland produced more varied responses among cartoonists than internment and the interrogation techniques which followed it. Cartoonists often charged Britain with hypocrisy over internment, and pointed to its exclusive use against Catholics. On interrogation methods, too, many overseas cartoonists saw little difference between Britain and some South American military dictatorships, and pointed to judgements by Amnesty International and the European Court of Human Rights to support their

and combat jackets introduced mainly by loyalist paramilitaries had been gratefully adopted. This sartorial confusion was gently mocked by Mahood. An old-guard IRA man, complete with trench coat, was confronting his son, sharply dressed in the latest fashion and holding a rifle: 'Jasus, Sean! You can't go out to murder people dressed like that' (*Punch*, August 18 1971). Cookson was also amused by paramilitary regalia, and drew a series of cartoons around the theme of dark glasses, called 'When Irish eyes are hiding': one man is decorated for losing a lens in Kilburn, and a potential recruit is told by a paramilitary officer, 'And when you've been in the service six months you're promoted to the heavy horn-rimmed kind' (*Punch*, June

"*My good fellow, you're allowed to scream only under torture! This is merely 'inhuman treatment' so pull yourself together*".

view. Particularly scathing criticisms were reserved for British official inquiries, like the Parker and Compton reports, which refused to condemn the interrogation techniques unconditionally. The Compton report, which attempted to distinguish between ill-treatment and torture, was regarded as sophistry by Drake of the *Irish Times* and by the *Socialist Challenge*.

19 1974). For most cartoonists, however, it was impossible to find any humour in the IRA. In the popular press particularly, the stereotype was very hostile, and the characteristic qualities of the IRA were their subhumanity, paganism and bloodymindedness.

It was a bloodymindedness which was applied rather indiscriminately. Few attempts were made to distinguish between the different republican and loyalist groups which proliferated during the early 1970s. Even during the bloody war between the Official and Provisional IRAs, there was little indication from cartoonists that their views were different, and the Official IRA bombings at Aldershot were taken as further confirmation. A similar lack

of interest applied to loyalist groups: all were lumped together as the mad Irish, and no distinctions made between their behaviours. In Cookson's cartoons about dark glasses, for example, it is not clear whether the actors were republican or loyalist, and it clearly did not matter very much. At the same time, there was a growing willingness to attribute the terror, bombing and murders to the Irish in general, rather than to paramilitary activists. A 'Historical Teach-in on Ireland', printed in the *Daily Mirror* on August 18 1969, contained this analysis: 'The Irish agree on one thing only. That is to go on arguing and fighting about a peace that has not existed in their history.' As the violence worsened, this also became the dominant analysis of the

Trog/*Observer*

Northern Irish problem by cartoonists.

Running counter to this view was a concern among journalists and cartoonists about the picture of the conflict which was being presented to the British public. Journalists like Simon Winchester of the *Guardian* and Bob Fisk of *The Times* were particularly worried about the stranglehold on news which had been acquired by the Army Information Office, and by the general lack of criticism of the army in the media. By its control of information about violent incidents, the army succeeded in defining the violence within a security context which was sympathetic to itself. The result was a remarkably uniform presentation of news, especially in the popular papers,

The recommendation in the Bennett Report of 1979 that closed circuit TV be installed to monitor interrogations was greeted by Cormac in *An Phoblacht* with something less than rejoicing. Compton also aroused misgivings for some British cartoonists. Horner and Trog suggested that the report amounted to a cover-up, and very few British cartoonists actually supported the government on the issue; Cummings in the *Daily Express* suggested that such concern for suspected terrorists was misplaced, and should more properly be applied to soldiers who had been their victims. Mahood also referred to the torture theme, but in a carefully jocular manner. However, the shortage of cartoons on these emotive issues may reflect a level of embarassment or confusion among British cartoonists. It certainly highlights one point: if cartoons are to be examined for the light they may throw on political attitudes, it is at least as important to look for the omitted themes as for those which appear in print.

"My sympathy, soldier! I'm just off to make sure that the chaps who may have killed you aren't being badly treated"

Cummings/Daily Express

"I'm afraid Mr. O'Connery can't come to the phone right now—he's having round-the-clock talks with our Intelligence section."

Mahood/Punch

and one which was rarely critical of the army. In 1973 Simon Hoggart summed it up: 'The PR exercise remains a considerable success. Hardly a word is breathed against the army in the popular papers or on radio and television in Britain' (*New Society*, October 11 1973). Two incidents during this period demonstrate the difficulties facing British newspapers and their cartoonists in covering a story which, while taking place in the United Kingdom, was treated more like a foreign war. They were Internment and the allegations of torture which accompanied it, and Bloody Sunday.

The general reaction to the introduction of Internment in August 1971 was muted. Few cartoonists treated the subject, and those who did mainly supported it as a reluctant necessity. It was not long before rumours began to circulate about interrogation techniques used by the army, including sensory deprivation, sonic hum and hooding. These charges were dismissed by virtually all the popular newspapers, despite three different official reports during the following year, all of which confirmed that there had been some level of ill-treatment. Among the publications which took the charges more seriously—notably the *New Statesman*, the *Sunday Times* and the *Morning Star*—there were two levels of response. The first was simply an expression of concern that the British army allowed such practices, and a degree of cynicism at the sophistry of the Compton Report, with its distinction between ill-treatment and torture. Horner's cartoon, with Humpty Compton sitting on a wall against which an internee was spreadeagled, had the caption, 'Brutality?... When I use a word it means just what I choose it to mean— neither more nor less' (*New Statesman*, November 26 1971).

The second level of concern was that pressure by Tory backbenchers for control of Northern Ireland's news, and the Compton and Parker reports, which accepted the occasional need for harsh interrogation techniques in exceptional circumstances, amounted to a cover-up. Both Horner in the *New Statesman* and Scarfe in the *Sunday Times* produced cartoons which drew a parallel between the hooding of suspects and hoodwinking the press (November 26 and November 21 1971). Horner's cartoons during this period consistently questioned official army statements. In a series printed between March 19 and December 3 1971, Internment was presented as a coup for Brian Faulkner, and as a prop for a privileged Stormont regime, which he depicted as a Frankenstein's monster. A particularly powerful cartoon had a soldier surveying an empty street, with blocked-up windows and black flags outside every house; the caption was a quotation from a recent army statement—'The army is winning the war in Northern Ireland' (February 4 1972).

These doubts, however, were quite out of step with the general reaction. Torture was rarely a theme in cartoons. Even in *Private Eye* it was completely ignored, and the *Observer*'s reputation for radicalism did not appear to extend to this issue. Only the redoubtable Mahood managed to find a funny side to it: a hooded prisoner is spreadeagled against a wall while an army officer answers the phone, 'I'm afraid Mr O'Connery can't come to the phone right now—he's having round-the-clock talks with our intelligence section' (*Punch*, May 23 1973).

In the popular press, the response to the torture allegations was much more aggressive. A cartoon in the *Express* by Cummings even incensed the *Mirror* to the point of an editorial attack: the cartoon showed a contemptuous Harold Wilson throwing a wreath on top of a dead soldier as he walked into an Internment camp, and saying 'My sympathy, soldier! I'm off to make sure that the chaps who may have killed you aren't being badly treated' (*Express*, October 20 1972). Nevertheless Cummings' stance reflected the attitude of cartoonists like Franklin in the *Sun*, Jak in the *Evening Standard*, and indeed most of the cartoonists in the popular dailies. The issue was regarded, when treated at all, as essentially one of perspective. Were the means being adopted by the army necessary to defeat the IRA? The answer was an almost unanimous Yes.

The events of Bloody Sunday, January 30 1972, when 13 people were killed by the army during a march in Derry, caused greater problems for cartoonists. In the first place, the incident took place under the eyes of massive television and press coverage, so there was immediate scepticism about the army's initial statement that the victims were IRA gunmen. Once again cartoonists in the popular papers were reluctant to contradict the supportive stance which they had taken previously by criticising the army, and played the incident down. It was left to those in more serious publications to express concern: Gibbard drew a conference table resting precariously on thirteen coffins, arranged as 'Steps towards a final settlement' (*Guardian Weekly*, February 5 1972). John Bierman in the *Listener* may have found the main explanation for the unwillingness of most cartoonists to express similar misgivings:

> I do believe that the English, being the least nationalistic people in the world, largely fail to understand the depth and intensity of Irish nationalist sentiment (and of Ulster Protestant patriotism, come to that) so that decent, liberal-minded Englishmen can say that 'it served the beggars right for being out marching when they should have obeyed the law and stayed at home'. Perhaps that particular

banality sums up the 800 years of mutual incomprehension that constitute the English presence in Ireland. (*Listener,* April 27 1972)

It was a banality which provided the moral of most cartoons about Bloody Sunday.

Hopes Dashed: March 1972–May 1974

Political and constitutional experiments were a main feature of the two years following the abolition of Stormont. Direct Rule had been intended as a temporary expedient until a local agreement could be reached, and plans seemed on course when three of the main parties met in conference at Darlington and agreed to cooperate in a Power-sharing Executive in 1974. Its fall, following the loyalist Ulster Workers' Council (UWC) strike, led to a reluctant resumption of Direct Rule. During all this violence continued at a high level, loyalist paramilitary groups became more active, and IRA violence spread to Britain.

The switch of emphasis to politics was reflected in the cartoons which were printed in British publications. With almost desperate relief, cartoonists adopted William Whitelaw, the Secretary of State for Northern Ireland, as the great new hope. The *Spectator* cartoonist Williams was particularly confident: 'Where there's a Willie there's a way', he claimed with more optimism than foresight (April 1 1972); in the same magazine a cover caricature by Willson, perhaps anticipating Operation Motorman by three weeks, showed a firm-jawed Whitelaw bursting into Free Derry like a determined Superman (July 8 1972). Trog, another admirer, cast Whitelaw in the role of the patently honest and decent English country gentleman, confident that goodwill and ingenuity would produce a solution; he was shown altering graffiti by moonlight, replacing 'Remember the Boyne' with 'Forget the Boyne' (*Punch,* July 5 1972). Frustrating him in his struggle against intolerance were both republican and loyalist terrorists: Garland represented Whitelaw, as usual the epitome of bemused reason, tied to a stake and tarred and feathered by the joint ministrations of the IRA and UDA (*New Statesman,* July 14 1972).

It was Whitelaw's good fortune to leave Ulster before the fall of the Executive which he had done so much to create, and his love affair with cartoonists and the press in general elevated him to the status of a leading, albeit unsuccessful, candidate for the Tory party leadership. The Executive itself was approved by cartoonists, but its prospects of survival were not rated highly. When it fell, some cartoons reflected a gloomy satisfaction that their pessimism had been justified, and that the Irish had confirmed their essential contrariness. In a Cummings cartoon, Edward Heath simply hoped that Ireland would disappear. The theme was revived by Osbert Lancaster in the same newspaper after the UWC strike. 'The trouble with Ireland', mused one of his characters, 'is that it's above sea level' (*Express*, July 11 1972; May 30 1974).

The continuing IRA campaign offered few novelties for cartoonists in Britain, and the tit-for-tat killings which were one of its main manifestations during the period were almost totally ignored—perhaps regarded as internal mysteries, too complex to merit attention. A sharp contrast was provided by their reactions to the extension of the IRA campaign to British cities. Calman's

The Irish in Britain

When the Republican bombing campaigns crossed the Irish sea they produced feelings of bitterness among the British and considerable embarrassment for the Irish who had made their homes in Britain. This was a far from insignificant group; in the 1966–70 Labour government, for example, 35 of the 363 Labour members of Parliament claimed Irish descent. Many had lived in Britain for generations, and were presented with conflicts of loyalty by the bombs and by the anti-Irish hostility they had aroused. 'To be brought up as an Irish Catholic in England', in the words of the writer John O'Callaghan, 'is to be nurtured as a schizophrenic'.

Mahood/*Punch*

"I still say they all protest too much."

Mahood/*Punch*

"I think this chap's call should have priority—he has an Irish accent!"

comment on the 1975 London bombs was a headstone marked 'Tomb of the Unknown Bystander' (*Sunday Times*, September 7 1975). The main change in the popular press was a greater tendency to blame the Irish rather than the IRA, although one new theme did emerge: the plight of the Irish who lived in Britain attracted some attention, and considerable sympathy. Mahood, himself an Ulsterman who had moved to London, cleverly caught the mixture of Irish guilt and English suspicion in a series of cartoons entitled, 'If you're Irish—What are you doing about it?' (*Punch*, March 21 1973): in one, a couple were having their baby rechristened: 'Sean, Patraig, Eamonn, I now rechristen you Edward, Harold, Jeremy...'; in another, two English under-

"Rooney, Ryan, Macnally and Kelly will continue to do the blasting but I've taken on Fetherstonhaugh here to hold the key to the gelly store."

Mahood/Punch

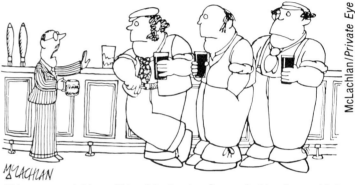

"Listen, you stinking rabble of Papist pigs, I'm not looking for trouble."

McLachlan/Private Eye

Mahood, the *Punch* cartoonist most interested in the plight of the Irish in England, pinpointed the two main responses—guilt and apprehension from the Irish, and suspicion from their English neighbours. Nevertheless, there was a benign undertone in his and McLachlan's cartoons, and even Raymond's wry comment on how the image of the stage Irishman had altered showed no real venom.

"Oh yes, he's your typical stage Irishman."

Raymond/Punch

takers were reading a tombstone on which was inscribed, 'I am not now, and never have been, a member of the IRA or the UDA or the rest of that ilk'; one says to the other, 'I still say they all protest too much'. Pubs were a favourite setting, not surprisingly as half of London's 8,000 pubs were managed or controlled by Irishmen, and so were building sites. Another of Mahood's cartoons had a foreman address a group of navvies thus: 'Rooney, Ryan, McNally and Kelly will continue to do the blasting, but I've taken on Fethers-tonhaugh here to hold the key to the gelly store' (*Punch*, March 21 1973). Although Mahood has been criticised elsewhere for anti-Irish bias (Kirkaldy, 1981), his cartoons stood as a contrast to the growing tendency among cartoonists in Britain to portray all the Irish as gun-loving hoodlums, and either overt or silent supporters of terror.

An Acceptable Level of Violence: May 1974-1983

A cartoon by Colin Wheeler in 1975 neatly encapsulated the continuing violence in Northern Ireland, its occasional outburst in Britain and the British tendency to explain it as simply a manifestation of inherent Irish abnormality: an IRA man listens to a phone message—'This is a police recording. Thank you for your bomb hoax call. Your nearest psychiatric hospital is at…' (*Private Eye*, September 12 1975). The years following the fall of the power-sharing Executive, barren of new political initiatives, settled down to a familiar and apparently hopeless chronicle of killings, bombs and acrimony. Direct Rule, originally conceived as a temporary expedient, began to assume a look of permanence, and a solution seemed further away than ever. The few cartoons which appeared in British publications during this period had a hackneyed and stilted aspect. Doves of peace, skeletons and bullying terrorists became repetitive images of a revulsion which cartoonists found difficult to convey effectively. Cummings castigated the courts for leniency towards the IRA, and the government of the Irish Republic for providing a haven for terrorists. Alongside a row of graves for the casualties in the feud between the Provisional and Official IRAs, Mahood drew an open grave and a tombstone above it inscribed 'Watch this space' (*Punch*, December 10 1975).

Some cartoonists were thinking longingly of British withdrawal from Northern Ireland as early as 1974. This was rarely articulated as more than a hearty desire to evacuate a brutal madhouse, such as that described in a serious British magazine by Paul Johnson in 1975:

> In Britain, as well as in Ulster, we face in the IRA not a nationalist movement, not

a league of patriots, not 'guerrillas' or 'freedom fighters', or anything which can be dignified with a political name, but an organisation of psychopathic murderers who delight in maiming and slaughtering the innocent and whose sole object and satisfaction in life is the destruction of human flesh (see Elliott 1976, 5: 18).

The desire to leave such monsters to their own devices was tempting. In 1974 Wheeler showed a soldier asking his mate, as bullets flew over their heads, 'Don't you realise we're here to stop the civil war that's going on from starting?'. Seven months later, he drew a scene outside an operating theatre, with one blood-covered surgeon informing another, 'The Government won't get out of Ireland in case there's a bloodbath' (*Private Eye*, April 19 and November 29 1974). Both cartoons challenged the main argument against withdrawal—that a civil war would follow—by suggesting that matters could hardly get worse than they were.

The number of cartoons about Northern Ireland in British publications diminished dramatically during this period. If the *Sunday Times, Express, Punch* and the *New Statesman* are taken as a representative cross-section of British publications, the number of cartoons about Northern Ireland fell from a total of 60 in 1972 to five in 1978. Only exceptional events, like the Papal visit to Ireland in 1979, and Ian Paisley's opposition to it, disturbed the general apathy. Keith Waite in the *Daily Mirror* showed Paisley blockading Ulster with barbed wire against a papal incursion, and McLachlan in the same paper had Paisley and an IRA man jointly bemoaning the possibility of the visit leading to an end of the violence (*Mirror*, July 23 1979).

Another personality with Ulster interests who caught the attention of cartoonists was Enoch Powell. In the *New Statesman*, the wide belief that Powell regarded Northern Ireland as a springboard for his assault on the Tory party leadership produced a Garland cartoon of Evel Powell preparing his motor bike for a jump from Belfast to Westminster (September 6 1974). 'If Enoch could come up with a policy for the repatriation of the Irish', one of Mahood's MPs speculated to another, 'the leadership would be his' (*Punch*, February 5 1975). A speech by Powell in 1978 warning against Prince Charles' marriage to a Roman Catholic earned the enmity of even Cummings: an IRA man observes Powell, drawn as a bomb and about to ignite the fuse, and says to his companion, 'You've got to admit, Paddy, Mr Powell is now more Irish than the Irish' (*Sunday Express*, December 10 1978). At least part of Powell's attraction to cartoonists was that his holding the Unionist seat for South Down allowed them to combine two distasteful targets in a single cartoon.

British Cartoons and Northern Ireland

The most striking feature of the British political cartoons about Northern Ireland is their remarkable conformity. On industrial relations, economic policy, even immigration, cartoons reflected the wide variety of popular views, but on Northern Ireland radical differences were rare. Philip Elliott noted the same phenomenon in the English press in general, and attributed it to the bipartisan policy on Northern Ireland shared by the three main British parties, which removed the issue from the arena of political dispute:

> The news media in Britain are very dependent on the parliamentary system and inter-party debate to air political issues and policies. When party conflict is removed, as it has been on Ulster policy since Northern Ireland came under direct rule, the scope for handling such issues within a news format is much reduced (Elliott 1976, 3: 7).

It was as if no editor wished to jeopardise the chances of a resolution of the conflict by treating it as the normal political free-for-all rough house. The rarity of deviance is an impressive illustration of the relationship between politics and the press in Britain.

This is not to suggest that there were not different political viewpoints. Cartoons in the *Spectator, Evening Standard* and *Express*, for example, are more conservative and chauvinistic than most, and the *Observer, New Statesman* and *Guardian* are more likely to express concern about such issues as media censorship, interrogation methods and the army. The point is that the continuum of views on Northern Ireland is more narrow than on other issues, and that it has tilted further towards the right with each year. The Conservative press unswervingly supported the bipartisan approach, and supported official policy regardless of the party in power. Any opposition, even at its most extreme, would more accurately be described as liberal rather than radical. The *New Statesman* provides an example. Its cartoonists voiced the most consistent criticism of any mainstream British publication, apart from the Communist *Morning Star*. Almost without exception, however, its most antagonistic cartoons were confined to the pre-1972 period and were directed against the indigenous Stormont administration; the distaste did not end with the coming of Direct Rule, but Whitelaw and Rees were not attacked with the same venom as Faulkner had been.

One way of testing the level of political uniformity is by examining the reactions of cartoonists to changes in government in Britain, especially in newspapers which supported the policies of opposition parties. The Conservative party, after all, had formal links with the Ulster Unionists and, given that 35 of the 363 Labour MPs in the 1966–70 Wilson government claimed Irish descent, there was some expectation that they would have greater sympathy with the nationalist cause. In the event, it is difficult to detect any significant difference of approach by cartoonists on the basis of prevailing governments. The only variable which seriously affected their interpretation was the personality or style of the Secretary of State for Northern Ireland at any time. William Whitelaw and Roy Mason were popular with cartoonists; they were sharply defined characters with policies appropriate both to their public characters and the mood of the times: Whitelaw was the tall honest peacemaker of the Darlington talks, Mason the small hard man who was going to smash the terrorists. By comparison, Merlyn Rees, Francis Pym and Humphrey Atkins were featureless and dull; they held little interest for cartoonists. In all cases, however, it was the politician's charisma rather than his political affiliation which determined the cartoonists' approach.

Naturally it is the cartoonists themselves, and their individual idiosyncrasies, who principally determined the theme and approach of their cartoons. While the relationship between a cartoonist and his publication varies greatly in each case, in general it is the employer who provides the political stage and backcloth—with the restraints which these imply—and the cartoonist who provides the themes and actors for the plays. Thus the *Sunday Express* can accommodate happily two such regular cartoonists as Giles and Cummings: Giles provides a softer, humorous and humane observation on current affairs, and Cummings a more uncompromising and polemical viewpoint; neither is likely to offend the conservative political line of the *Sunday Express*, and neither has.

At the same time, most cartoonists are attracted to particular themes of their own, and coverage of Northern Ireland in different publications was at least as likely to depend on the cartoonist's interest in the subject as on editorial policy. Garland in the *New Statesman* produced anti-Stormont cartoons during 1970 and 1971, when few others did. Mahood, who spent his first twenty-five years in Belfast, was the major reason for *Punch*'s preoccupation with the issue; he had no obvious commitment to either side in the conflict, but his emphasis on the bigotry and violence in Ireland was informed by his knowledge of the complexities of the issue. Colin Wheeler in *Private Eye* seemed to regard it merely as another setting for his humour, while Jak of the *Evening Standard* and Cummings of the *Express* presented a strongly committed picture of British fairmindedness and Irish psychopathy. In contrast to these different levels of interest in Northern Ireland stand most British cartoonists, whose occasional comments on the subject arose either from editorial suggestion or an extraordinary incident. In general, cartoons on Northern Ireland which appeared in British publications support the view that the cartoonist's interest is the main determinant of the subject of his cartoons; however, the two are rarely if ever in conflict.

It is instructive to compare the themes favoured by cartoonists with the patterns of violence in the province. The comparison is more interesting for omissions than inclusions. Riots, bombs, the IRA, the army and political initiatives account for the great majority of cartoons. The sectarian murders, which were a main concern in Northern Ireland, particularly from 1972 to 1974, were almost totally ignored. Internment too was clearly an embarrassment for some liberal cartoonists; those who treated it at all contented themselves with either accepting it as a necessary evil, or pointed to the contradictory British policies on internment in Ulster and Rhodesia. It might have been imagined too that the criticism of army interrogation methods by bodies ranging from Amnesty International to the European Court of Human Rights, not to mention the semantic juggling of the Compton and Parker reports, would have provided rich pickings for cartoonists; in fact it was not a popular theme. These omissions were all the more striking when compared with cartoons printed outside Britain: the very subjects which were underplayed or neglected in Britain accounted for the overwhelming majority of cartoons relating to Ulster which appeared in European and North American newspapers.

The main reason for the neglect of these subjects, and the popularity of others, appears to lie in the level of British political and emotional investment in the province. The arrival of the army in Northern Ireland in August 1969 was a critical turning point. Until that time Northern Ireland was regarded by most cartoonists in Britain as a curious if repellant place, close enough to merit interest, but alien enough to dispel any guilt about British responsibility for events there. It was treated as a foreign war rather than an internal dispute within the United Kingdom—a Vietnam rather than a Toxteth. The change following the army's arrival was subtle, but fundamental. It was still treated as a foreign war, but one towards which there was no longer neutrality: if the army was there, soon to be followed by Direct Rule, its opponents must be either evil or misguided. So the rioters, who had been merely amusing or quaint, were converted into IRA gunmen long before reality caught up with the cartoonists' imagination. In effect, the entry of the army increased British emotional investment in Northern Ireland, and it became as unnatural for cartoonists to criticise it as it had been during the Hitler war. Even though the enemy was technically operating within the

United Kingdom, there was little disagreement that Britain was at war, and the conventions and atmosphere of war are not conducive to dissent.

If the analogy with a foreign war is extended, another consequence is the development of a hostile stereotype of the enemy, and the view of Northern Ireland from England became increasingly hostile. Undoubtedly the Provisional IRA were the universally agreed enemy, but few cartoonists in Britain found anything in the province with which to sympathise; there was a discernable ripple effect of general antipathy towards the Ulster people, and indeed the Irish. The fine tuning required to explain the complexities of the conflict were frequently sacrificed for a broad but simple picture of blood, violence and depression. All the paramilitaries, loyalist and republican, were tarred with the same brush. Their internecine feuds and retaliatory killings seemed indistinguishable, and perhaps not worth distinguishing.

So the cartoons about Northern Ireland which have appeared in the British press portray the province as the cuckoo in the United Kingdom nest. Even when the violence was at its peak, Northern Ireland never reached the status of a major issue in British politics. The Irish sea provided a psychological as well as a physical barrier to the spread of disorder to the British mainland. 'Ireland is no longer, as it once was, at the centre of vision of any substantial section of British society', wrote Sarah Nelson in 1976. 'It is still a problem... but one to be dispensed with rather than understood, for any sense of shared identity is almost gone' (Nelson, 1976). Her point is confirmed by the cartoonists' treatment of the violence, and particularly of the province's politicians. Only when their actions impinged directly on British politics were they considered at all, and then only as occasional players. The main actors in political cartoons were almost exclusively British, although the Prime Ministers of the Irish Republic, as heads of a sovereign state, were accorded equal status; Jack Lynch may have been unpopular with British cartoonists, but none of them doubted that he had a role in the drama. On the other hand, only those Northern Irish politicians who had progressed from provincial repertory to the Westminster stage, like Paisley, Fitt and Devlin, were thought to be worth consideration. Apart from Brian Faulkner, who was regarded for a time as a potential saviour, the Northern Irish politicians who operated in the province were either ignored by cartoonists, or shown as fractious, petty and essentially irrelevant. Thus the stereotypes of incompetent leaders complemented the more general image of the violent, psychotic Irish, and the analysis of the Troubles was complete.

The Home Front:

Cartoonists in Ireland

3

I can only express good by a comparison between evil and greater evil.
Gerald Scarfe

IRELAND, north and south, has not provided a climate suitable for cartoonists since the advent of partition. *Dublin Opinion*, a political weekly which had begun publication in 1922, kept the art form alive against difficult odds, but eventually abandoned the struggle in 1956. The problem lay in the absence of the pool of cartoonists which a more supportive daily press might have provided. As a result, Irish cartoonists were forced either to seek markets and themes outside Ireland, or to regard cartooning as a part-time activity. So the situation remains today. In the entire island there is only one cartoonist, Martyn Turner of the *Irish Times*, contracted to an Irish newspaper on a full-time basis. The rest rely on freelance earnings or more limited contracts. So, when Northern Ireland emerged as a major political issue in 1969, there were few Irish cartoonists ready to take advantage of it. Despite this, the cartoons printed in Ireland during the following twelve years illustrate important and unique aspects of the conflict; they also reveal the vastly different perspectives of the violence on the two sides of the Irish border.

Northern Ireland

The pattern of newspaper publishing in Northern Ireland demonstrates vividly the pre-eminence of economic over political interests, when the two are in conflict. The province has two daily morning newspapers, one Sunday newspaper and one evening newspaper. The two morning papers, in direct competition, cater frankly for sectarian readerships; the *Irish News* provides a steady diet of nationalist politics and Catholic social and religious events for a 93% Catholic readership, and the *Newsletter* a similar range of Unionist-Orange news for its readers, 87% of whom are Protestant. Neither the *Sunday News* nor the *Belfast Telegraph*, on the other hand, is faced with competition, and their news coverage and political stances reflect their more eclectic readership. In addition to these newspapers, the liberal magazine *Fortnight* was published regularly between 1970 and 1976, and thereafter on a bewilderingly irregular basis. During its first six years *Fortnight*'s joint editor was a cartoonist, and the magazine was an outlet for almost 200 cartoons, among them some of the most penetrating and perceptive comments to appear anywhere in the world. Apart from *Fortnight*, however, there were few opportunities for Ulster's cartoonists. The *Belfast Telegraph* has published a weekly cartoon by Rowel Friers, but few have appeared on the pages of the *Irish News* or the *Newsletter*. As for the *Sunday News*, a

Police, Prosecutions and Prisons

Evening all. Mind how you go on the roads . . .

Horner/*New Statesman*

During a period of growing unemployment and economic recession, two groups within Northern Ireland's population expanded dramatically. The Royal Ulster Constabulary, including reserves, rose from 3,044 in 1969 to 9,721 in 1975, and the prison population from 727 to 2,848 during a similar six-year period. Police, courts and prisons had all been centres of controversy even before the Troubles started, and became more popular as themes for Irish cartoonists after 1968. Outside the province they were clearly regarded as obscure and provincial concerns, and rarely featured in cartoons.

Horner's suspicion of the Royal Ulster Constabulary in the 1969 *New Statesman* cartoon, therefore, was exceptional. The reaction of Northern Irish cartoonists to the police reflected vested interests: the inability of the R.U.C. to patrol some republican districts, for example, was a favourite theme for both Oisin of the

short-lived attempt to include political cartoons was hastily abandoned when some controversial themes were considered potentially offensive to the paper's ecumenical, or at any rate cross-denominational, readers. These themes included a bottle in Paddy Devlin's hand and a notice on the Stormont notice board reading 'No shooting, no spitting, no Republicans', both of which were blacked out of cartoons by Martyn Turner. Another, with Brian Faulkner saying, 'It's about time I made a gesture to the minority', and the silhouette of his fingers showing clearly what the gesture was, was not printed by the *Sunday News*, but found a ready market in the *Irish Times*, south of the border. The Northern media, however, could hardly be described

Oisin/*Andersonstown News*

BACK ON THE BEAT !!!

Rowel Friers

FALLS RD.

Andersonstown News and Rowel Friers of the *Belfast Telegraph*, but their responses were rather different. It is fair to say, however, that neither viewed the prospects of a return to regular policing in such irregular times with a great deal of optimism.

The courts provided a much more fruitful subject. Apart from allegations of Unionist bias among the judiciary, there was considerable criticism of the extent to which due process of law had been jettisoned as violence increased. Blame was attached in roughly equal propor-

tions to the intimidation of witnesses by paramilitary groups and to the introduction of internment and non-jury trials by the government. In 1973 Martyn Turner neatly demonstrated the complications inherent in permitting Special Category status, which gave loyalist and republican prisoners considerable control over their

as cartooning nursery slopes.

Despite this, the Troubles have been the subject of some outstanding cartoons. Rowel Friers, the *Belfast Telegraph*'s Saturday cartoonist, had been producing drawings since the days of *Dublin Opinion*, but his themes and treatments were strongly affected by the violence of the 1970s. An Ulsterman, he is one of the few cartoonists to catch successfully the character and accent of his countrymen, and his interest in their vernacular is unique. During the 1950s and 1960s most of his cartoons were universal rather than provincial in nature, with an attraction towards featuring pirates, sportsmen and Mexican cowboys in amusing, but quite apolitical, settings.

"Biased!! How dare you, you long haired Fenian agitator."

"The case for the defence, your honour, on this ludicrous arms charge, is that if you commit them for trial, they'll blow your brains out."

own affairs; he highlighted a real case, when a Shankill man convicted of rape asked for the privileged status of Political Prisoner on the grounds that the girls were Catholic.

Even the abused R.U.C. found humour in

With the onset of the Troubles Friers, a gifted caricaturist, concentrated initially on Ulster politics, and followed its issues and characters with a tolerance and affection which cut across the sectarian spectrum. These were his people and his view of them was characteristically benign. Censure was reserved for the IRA, UDA and those who used violence; it was rarely personified. Like the *Belfast Telegraph*, in which most of his cartoons appeared, the cartoons adopted a liberal reformist stance, with particular soft spots for Brian Faulkner, Gerry Fitt and William Whitelaw. His more critical cartoons were all the more effective because of their infrequency. 'We shall

Police Beat

the administration of justice. In a rare political comment in *Police Beat*, it is ironically suggested that allegations of torture in Castlereagh barracks may have

Martyn Turner/Fortnight

"Peace on Earth, Goodwill to all Men and Hang the Terrorists"

been exaggerated. For Martyn Turner's respectable Ulsterman, torture would have been too humane. It was left to Dobson, however, to produce a classic cartoon by taking the standard republican courtroom declaration, 'I refuse to recognise the court', and introducing a small but powerful twist.

Dobson/Fortnight

'I refuse to recognise the inside of this cell'

overcome' showed Civil Rights marchers stamping over the heads of judges and lawyers, but the marchers are clearly respectable and well-intentioned (*Fortnight*, November 20 1970). In 1974 a strong cartoon represented Merlyn Rees, the Secretary of State for Northern Ireland, as a puppet on the knee of a general, but much of the strength comes from its contrast with Friers' other cartoons—as if the Pope had lost his temper in public. Paralleling these political comments ran a series of well drawn and rather formal cartoons attacking the prevalence of both republican and loyalist violence: a loyalist hoodlum, club in hand, triumphantly holds up the body of a dove after the 1974 UWC strike; IRA leaders are shown enjoying their ill-gotten gains in the lap of luxury. Alongside these depressing and increasingly hopeless images, however, Friers presented a more appealing picture of the Ulster character—honest folk trying to live decent lives in the midst of murder and bombs. Friers is the cartoonist closest to the conflict, and the one most affected by it.

Martyn Turner inherited the theme. He is English, and was joint editor of *Fortnight* and occasional cartoonist for the *Sunday News* before his abrupt dismissal. A fine caricaturist, Turner's contempt for politicians is located in an older tradition of political cartooning, and contrasts with Friers' more sympathetic portrayals. His cynicism towards politicians has not been softened by their requests for his most critical cartoons; the original of one cartoon concerning a police raid on the UDA headquarters, with the para-militaries attacking the police as 'non-sectarian lackeys', was requested by both organisations. Between 1970 and 1976, when Turner worked in Northern Ireland, the conflict dominated his cartoons, and they come closest to providing a satirical and knowledgeable commentary on contempory Irish affairs. Some of Northern Ireland's institutions provided his favourite settings. The courts, for example, were used to develop the themes of discrimination, bigotry and violence: a judge glowers down at a hapless prisoner and snarls, 'Biased!! How dare you, you long haired Fenian agitator' (*Fortnight*, May 14 1971); a barrister defending an IRA man in Dundalk No. 1 Court disclaims, 'The case for the defence, your honour, on this ludicrous arms charge, is that, if you commit them for trial, they'll blow your brains out' (*Fortnight*, February 23 1972). The churches, especially the Roman Catholic church, were another of Turner's favourite targets: on the Irish Republic's anti-contraception laws, he showed a priest asking, 'How can you parents possibly know as much about bringing up children as us priests?' These attacks on local institutions are rare. Apart from Turner, only Ralph Dobson, whose cartoons also appeared in *Fortnight*, surveyed the scene with a jaundiced eye. Dobson, a very talented but infrequent cartoonist, specialised in sharp political caricatures and cartoons, and drew what may be the best single cartoon on the Troubles: a play on the frequent IRA refusal to recognise Northern Irish courts, Dobson showed a prisoner squatting in his cell, with the caption, 'I refuse to recognise the inside of this cell' (*Fortnight*, October 15 1971).

The Northern Irish cartoons on local politics and the effects of violence on innocent people provide insights which are not found anywhere else. Outside the province, the naivety of many cartoons often arises from their willingness to present the violence without any context, thus providing an impression of unintelligible mayhem. If anything, the local cartoonists tend towards the opposite extreme and sometimes become bogged down in a welter of initials—UUUC, DUP, SDLP, UCDC and the rest. Indeed the complexity of provincial politics was a favourite theme; Turner showed a tattooist seeking space on a loyalist's arm on which to engrave the initials of the latest loyalist grouping, and commenting, 'Like the rest of us, young man, you won't be able to take much more of loyalist politics' (*Fortnight*, June 1976). Similarly with the other favourite theme, violence: Dobson, Friers and Turner all regarded the internal differences between loyalist and republican paramilitaries as minute when weighed against their common terrorism, but their accurate attribution of berets, dark glasses and combat jackets at least make it clear at any time which group they are attacking. Nevertheless there is an awareness of the dangers of overgeneralisation and an excess of outrage. On Christmas 1975 Turner pictured a plump, middle-aged man, Christmas cracker in hand, cigar in mouth and glass raised for the jovial toast, 'Peace on Earth, Goodwill to all men and Hang the Terrorists' (*Fortnight*, December 19 1975). The same cartoonist, in a reference to the alarming increase of young people in jail, presented a 'Portrait of a Terrorist', showing a young, bemused and unthreatening schoolboy (*Fortnight*, May 7 1976). It was their awareness that the issues were complex and their boundaries blurred that made it difficult for the Northern Irish cartoonists to deal with the issue of violence. All the cartoonists who featured in the conventional media were opposed to the use of force from all sides, although Turner was the only one to suggest that the British army was also part of the violence. In June 1972, for example, he showed Hitler as a school-master instructing his IRA and UDA pupils, 'Always call the game *preservation of law and order* or *protection of people's rights*—then you can get away with murder'; the third pupil in the class was a British soldier. Generally, however, on controversial issues like internment, torture and the army, criticism of the establishment by cartoonists was undercut by fear that trenchant attacks might give comfort to the paramilitaries.

Between 1969 and 1974 an analysis of cartoons printed in Northern Ireland might give the impression of an obsession with community conflict. In fact it demonstrates the intrusion of the conflict into almost every aspect of social policy and relationships. When commenting on education, justice, policing and general social issues, it was almost impossible to avoid their sectarian connotations. In observing this, the mainstream cartoonists adopted the role of the common Ulsterman, often featured in the cartoons as a mild, bewildered moderate; no bigot, he abhors the violence around him, but is

Stormont Agonistes

Martyn Turner/Fortnight

Northern Ireland's internal politics were too provincial and too complex to attract many cartoonists from outside Ulster. Even Irish cartoonists became increasingly disenchanted with nationalist defensiveness and the interminable splits within unionism. As a result, local politicians were rarely caricatured in cartoons unless, like Gerry Fitt and Ian Paisley, they had graduated from the

Stormont repertory theatre to Westminster stardom. Apart from these, the most effective cartoons were those which stereotyped political stances rather than personalities, like Martyn Turner's descriptions of the sorts of parliament demanded by the four main political groupings in 1971. Their common denominator was their reluctance to include the other three in their plans: even

forced into his sectarian trench by the venality of short-sighted politicians, insensitive clergy and brutal gunmen. Even when the Ulster politicians are abused, however, they are treated seriously. In contrast to some cartoons from outside Ulster, the complexity of the problem is given its proper due. Gunmen are distinguished from ordinary citizens, loyalists from republicans, the Officials from the Provisionals. In the middle stand, or sometimes lie in order to avoid bullets, the ordinary people, terrorised by violence, but increasingly accepting it as part of the environment; after all, they have to live in the place. Their reactions, therefore, lack the extravagance sometimes attributed to them by less knowledgeable cartoonists—war-weariness rather

Martyn Turner/*Fortnight*

Rowel Friers

"LIKE THE REST OF US, YOUNG MAN, YOU WON'T BE ABLE TO TAKE MUCH MORE OF LOYALIST POLITICS"

tolerance, far removed from Stormont's malevolent reality.

It was the loyalists who provided the favourite target. Their labyrinthine squabbles and plots, and bewildering array of acronyms, confused both the cartoonists and their own traditional supporters. Friers, for instance, sensed an unease among respectable Orangemen at finding themselves harnessed with loyalist paramilitaries.

than despair, resignation rather than depression. Life goes on, and the Troubles even provided their own form of self-effacing humour—'the joker in the pack that confuses the label stickers', according to the local humourist, Billy Simpson. Simpson himself poked fun at the sort of Ulster stereotype which was often presented outside the province:

> If you wanted to create a creature who approximates to the popular image you would have to build him from spare parts of the rest of us. A kind of bionic bigot. The Prod parts would comprise a dour agricultural Mr Barrett-of-Wimpole-Street who regards levity as a character flaw, and spending money as a breach of a Commandment that the good Lord

Dobson/Fortnight

'Have you considered what will happen to us when we run out of targets'

Cartoons about other parties were infrequent, perhaps because they lacked the political power to attract heavy artillery: the S.D.L.P. were merely a negative and irresponsible opposition; the D.U.P. was so dominated by Ian Paisley that it rarely appeared as a separate entity; as for the Alliance party, it suffered the inevitable fate of middle groups in a polarised political system, that of being regarded as well-meaning but ineffective ditherers.

forgot to write in. And the Gaelic touches would be more poetic, artistic, equally sullen and perpetually the worst for drink (Simpson, 1979).

The Northern Irish cartoonists, although prepared at times to adopt Simpson's burlesque stereotypes, were the only ones interested in examining their more complex undertones.

Although their treatment of the complexities reflected a more accurate reality, it did not present a clearer one. The more the cartoonists understood the motives of the protagonists, the more ineffectual their work. Unlike Rab from the *Loyalist News* and Cormac from the *Republican News*, Friers and Turner lacked an evangelical commitment and a single-minded focus for

AS EASY AS **1,2,3....**

Oisin/*Andersonstown News*

the middle-of-the-road Alliance party stood for a spurious holier-than-thou To Oisin in the *Andersonstown News*

the entire crew was dismissed contemptuously as colonialist pawns scrambling for Mr. Whitelaw's baubles.

Even for less committed cartoonists there were few heroes among Northern Ireland's politicians.

their attacks. Without these, their obsession with the conflict gradually abated. From 1974 the violence settled down to a dreary repetitive cycle of shootings, bombs and death, without even the shock of novelty. At the same time the resumption of Direct Rule after the collapse of the power-sharing Executive took away from the local cartoonists their stage and their actors. This combination of sterile violence and political stagnation deeply affected them: Dobson's output fell; Turner's move to the *Irish Times* in Dublin did not diminish his interest in the Northern conflict, but reduced it to the status of one string to his bow; Friers' Saturday cartoons in the *Belfast Telegraph* continue, but the proportion dealing with the conflict has fallen considerably. All of them know more about the Northern Irish conflict than any of the other cartoonists. In the end they were all left with very little new to say.

The Republic of Ireland

The larger population and greater number of newspapers in the Irish Republic have not provided the broader market for cartoonists that might have been expected. In the five daily newspapers published in Dublin alone, only one has a full-time cartoonist, although others regularly use freelance work. Among the small number of cartoons which they printed during the 1960s, however, it could not be claimed that Northern Ireland featured as a major concern. When it did, the cartoons often combined a vague aspiration towards Irish unification with a more uneasy concentration on the qualities which were thought to distinguish northerners from southerners—dourness, political bigotry, religious obsession and business skill.

When Martyn Turner moved to the Irish Times in 1976 he became the only full-time cartoonist in Ireland, north or south. Having come from Northern Ireland, he was both informed and interested in its conflict. Nevertheless, he was conscious of the risk of becoming obsessed with the theme, and his interests soon broadened to include Southern politics and European issues, reflecting the concerns of the newspaper. Despite this, he brought to Dublin an inside view of the effects of the violence on the Northern Irish community, and one which ran counter to the blander comments of some other Southern cartoonists.

Apart from Turner, a number of cartoonists had regular or frequent features in other newspapers and magazines. Francis Drake was his predecessor at the *Irish Times*, and also appeared in *Hibernia* magazine. His early references to Northern Ireland after 1969 were unremarkable, but a series of Northern caricatures in 1978, under his new pseudonym Littleman, were brilliant and devastating. *Hibernia* also printed the work of more conventional cartoonists like Jim Fitzpatrick and Jim Cogan. Fitzpatrick's cartoons in 1968 and 1969 reflected the popular southern view of Northern Ireland: Bill Craig, Northern Ireland's Minister of Home Affairs, was easily identified as the bully, and Bernadette Devlin as a saint (*Hibernia*, November 29 1968; April 25 1969). The hagiolatry of Bernadette was also an early feature of Cogan's cartoons, with Ian Paisley providing the necessary contrast. Ged, Doll and most of the other southern cartoonists subscribed to a similar outlook, although Froy, whose cartoons appeared in the *Sunday World* from 1973 until his untimely death in 1979, provided a more unpredictable and varied diet.

For some of these cartoonists publication was irregular and payment low. As late as 1979 Tom Mathews, whose cartoons appeared regularly in *In Dublin*, was paid £10 for each drawing (Doyle 1979). Not surprisingly, therefore, their output and approaches varied considerably. Their attitude to the Northern conflict, however, was remarkably uniform. In the first place, it caught their attention. The Civil Rights marches of 1968, and their resistance by the Unionist government and by the Royal Ulster Constabulary appeared to confirm stereotypes which were already well established in the Irish Republic. The struggle was an uncomplicated one between right and wrong; the Civil Rights marchers and Bernadette were on the side of the angels—she was drawn as a beautiful superwoman in a pure white mini-dress by Cogan, and as a stately Celtic queen, framed by Celtic scrolls, by Fitzpatrick. Craig and the Unionists, on the other hand, were bigoted, mean and violent. Ian Paisley in particular was treated as a music hall villain, Ged filling his massive mouth with tombstones and church spires instead of teeth. There was an undertone of ethnic stereotyping in some cartoons. Given Irish resentment at the British tendency towards racial caricature of the Irish, it is ironic that Ulster Protestants were sometimes represented in similar fashion by Southern cartoonists. 'Change lieders(sic) and we'll fight you all over again' was the curious caption of a cartoon by Cogan (*Hibernia*, April 13 1970); the cartoon showed a mini-skirted Bernadette surrounded by smiling open faces and, on the other side of a wall, a large bullying Paisley, supported by besashed, contorted bigots.

This familiar picture was not to last for long. The entry of the Provisional IRA to the scene and the growth of violence in the north complicated its simple outlines. Support for the ideal of Irish unification was not diminished, but the Provisionals' violent search for the same objective presented a serious dilemma for cartoonists: to attack the IRA campaign might be considered as giving comfort to the British government and the Ulster loyalists; to attack Britain too violently might suggest that they condoned the use of force. From about 1975 this dilemma was resolved by largely ignoring Northern Ireland and its complications, a process encouraged by a growing pessimism about political initiatives. When the subject was broached at all, it most often took the form of rather desultory attacks on British politicians and the perennial soft target of Ian Paisley, enthusiastically rediscovered during the Papal visit to Ireland in 1979. With few exceptions, the activities of the Provisional IRA were discreetly avoided. This disillusion with Northern Ireland is perhaps best traced by the treatment of Bernadette Devlin by Southern cartoonists, from the stylised heroine of 1969 to the frumpish harridan of Littleman's cruel 1978 caricature in *Hibernia.*

Beneath the change in Southern attitudes, from naivete to disillusion, lay an uneasy and persistent thread of apprehension that the violence might spill over the border. The view of the north by Southern cartoonists was often formed from a nervous glance over the shoulder. When the H-Blocks and hunger strikes issues came to the fore in 1980, Northern Ireland burst rudely into the foreground. Two IRA prisoners in Northern Ireland won seats in the Dail in 1981, and Dublin had its first taste of serious rioting in July of that year. The new concern was strongly represented in a *Sunday Tribune* cartoon by Quinn on August 9 1981: the intransigence of both hunger strikers and the British government was illustrated by a huge letter H, planted in Britain and Ireland, its two arms surmounted by Mrs Thatcher and a hunger striker; the deaths caused by the violence were represented by crosses on the Irish side of the picture and, significantly, the crosses were shown south of the border as well as north. However, apart from those occasions when Northern violence threatened Southern stability, interest in the North's violence was muted. Lip service to the ideal of a united island was almost universal, but there are few signs of absorption with the theme. The dominant impression of Southern cartoons about the North was that they were drawn from a sense of duty rather than commitment.

Perhaps the most surprising component of the cartoons, especially those printed between 1968 and 1970, was the remarkable ignorance of Northern Irish affairs which they revealed. Apart from the general orthodoxy of republicanism which underpinned most of them, there was no more evidence of any special knowledge of the province than may be found among British or overseas cartoonists. Their approach to the Northern vernacular was particularly revealing: 'Let's flush the blady Papists out', Cogan has a loyalist say in one of his cartoons; Ged, in a more ambitious attempt in the *Irish Times*, gives Paisley this speech: 'In God's name, willyas tak note of the big man this Twelfth'. These disastrous attempts to catch the cadences of the

Ulster accent, no more successful than the begorrahs and bhoys attributed to Ulstermen by some American and English cartoonists, not only reveal an ignorance of the north; more to the point, they reveal a willingness to stress the distinctions between Northerners and Southerners. The revival, or rather discovery, of real Southern involvement in the issue after the hunger strikes in 1981 further illustrate the point: throughout the 1970s the interest was not in Northern Ireland *per se*, but only in its potential to affect affairs in the Republic.

South of the Border

Dublin Opinion

Even before the Northern crisis erupted in 1968 the Southern establishment regarded Northern Ireland with a nice mixture of official lust and private revulsion. Cartoonists avoided the subject as best they could in the pages of *Dublin Opinion*. The 1935 Industrial map of Ireland, the border defended by Orange drums, revealed neither knowledge nor interest in what was going on behind it.

A similar remove accompanied the cartoons of the early 1970s. Almost all cartoonists in the Irish Republic identified with the Catholic minority in Northern Ireland, but mostly with little insight or commitment. There was one period, however, when Southern concern became almost agitation: during the hunger strikes of 1981, demonstrations and marches south of the border excited concern that the violence in Northern Ireland would spill over—a concern well caught in Quinn's cartoon in the *Sunday Tribune*, with one leg of its immense H, and tombstones, planted firmly in the Irish Republic.

North and South

The similarities and differences between cartoons printed in Northern Ireland and those printed in the Irish Republic reflect the similarities and distinctions between overlapping cultures. There are common sensitivities which unite the island, and local nuances which are discernably different on either side of the border. A concern about sex, or rather sexual candour, is general. Turner, while denying that he was subjected to political censorship by the *Irish Times*, conceded that sexual matters attracted the newspaper's disapproval (Doyle 1979). There is a similar sensitivity about

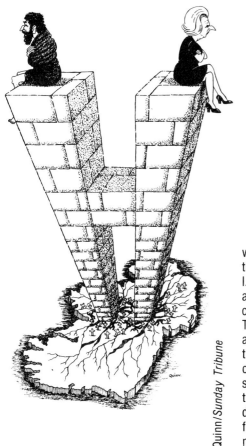

Quinn/*Sunday Tribune*

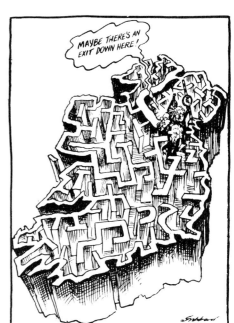

Gibbard/*Guardian*

The other Maze prison

British cartoonists, on the other hand, were often critical of the Republic's role in the conflict, accusing her of condoning the I.R.A. campaign by casual border vigilance and by her refusal to extradite political criminals.

The Thatcher-Haughey talks of 1980, which attempted to treat Northern Ireland within the broader context of international co-operation between two neighbouring states, produced a nicely ambiguous cartoon by Gibbard in the *Guardian*. Is this direct contact with the Republic a real exit for Britain from the Northern Irish maze, or merely an escape into another dead end?

alcohol, which may be more related to fear of law suits than morality. Turner has had the unique distinction of having bottles, clutched in the hands of well-known politicians, blocked out from cartoons in both parts of Ireland. The preoccupation with the evils of sex and booze is partly the product of a society with a remarkably high religiosity, and few cartoons aimed at the churches have appeared in Irish newspapers, although the more irreverent *Fortnight* and *Hibernia* have printed some.

The main difference between Northern and Southern cartoonists, however, lies in their commitment to the issue. There is concern about Northern Ireland among Southern cartoonists, but it is most often a generalised concern about abstract issues like justice and violence, or a detailed fear that the unrest might spread southwards and engulf their own community. In Northern Ireland the humour is more therapeutic and more intense. The violence pervaded almost every aspect of social contact, and left no-one untouched. The main problem for the Northern cartoonists was that knowledge blurred rather than sharpened the issues. Almost inevitably it became possible to appreciate, if not to support, the views of all sides. The result was that the conflict became obsessive for many Northern cartoonists, but it became increasingly difficult for them to respond to it. Unless he was committed to one or other of the extreme positions, it was almost impossible to deal with the daily chronicle of deaths and destruction. The cartoonists in the Republican and Loyalist publications had an easier task, and could strongly advocate their political objectives and attack their opponents. The more mainstream cartoonists, on the other hand, straddled a see-saw with a foot on either side. Extra support, or withdrawal of support, on either side could not be given a vacuum; to support one side was to oppose the other. Where this analogy fails is that it assumes that see-saws operate on a single dimension. For the cartoonist, the conflicting parties at varying times included different shades of republicans and loyalists, rival political parties, Britain, the British army, the Irish Republic and others. To attempt arbitration between such diverse interests eventually proved too demanding. By the mid-70s the vigour of the previous five years had largely dissipated.

Cartoonists at War:
Military and Paramilitary

4

Cartoons are more likely to be effective when the artist's attitude is hostile, to be even better when his attitude is rage, and when he gets to hate he can really get going.

Jules Feiffer

IT is one activity for a professional to draw cartoons about violence for daily newspapers, but quite another for an activist to illustrate the violence which he supports and which may eventually kill him. The crudest and most bitter cartoons fall into the latter category, but others give more surprising insights into the nature of motivation, propaganda and sectarianism.

This chapter deals with the cartoons produced at the front line of violence, by British soldiers, republicans and loyalist paramilitaries.

The British Army

'Barrack room cartoonists, like barrack room lawyers, have always been part of the British army life', claimed an article in *Visor*, 'and Northern Ireland has been no exception' (November 27 1977). Certainly the pages of *Visor*, a weekly newspaper for soldiers in Northern Ireland, started in 1974, confirm the view. Cartoons vied with regimental pin-ups for space, and few issues did not carry at least one cartoon. Three collections of cartoons originally printed in *Visor* were published as books and, to ensure that all ranks joined in the fun, cartoon competitions were held by the paper. 'You need not worry if your drawings are not up to the standard of Giles', the editor cajoled, usually unnecessarily, 'it's the humour that counts'. The result was that soldiers on active service in Northern Ireland produced more than 500 cartoons between 1974 and 1979, almost without exception relating to their own predicament.

Regiments stationed in Northern Ireland are not permanently posted there. They also spend periods of service in Britain, West Germany and other regions. Some of the army cartoons printed in Ulster could easily have appeared in newspapers published in these other bases, or indeed in the publication of any army. They deal in genre jokes about the soldier's unfortunate lot. The food is appalling; billets are dirty and cramped; and the squaddie, the innocent and passive hero of most cartoons, is expected to deal with a variety of tasks—fireman, policeman, driver—which would not be tolerated by a civilian. Amid all this squalor, the squaddie manages to keep his good humour. One soldier on a Belfast street fending off all kinds of missiles including (literally) the kitchen sink, remarks to another, 'And then my dad said "Why don't you join the army and stop standing around on street corners?"' (*Visor* May 9 1973)

This wry detached attitude to Northern Ireland's violence is perhaps the most consistent image presented by the soldiers of themselves. The cartoon squaddie finds the problem itself incomprehensible and the natives hostile. Not surprisingly he has no ideological involvement in the issues which have brought him to Ireland, and views both loyalist and republican rioters as indistinguishable and sharing the common objective of making life difficult for him. A 1974 squaddie, for example, stands innocently beneath a battered peace sign, flowers clutched in his hand, bullets flying all around him and speculates, 'Well it could be the Officials firing at Provos or the IRA firing at the Prots or the UDA firing at the Officials or the UVF firing at the Cats—on the other hand they could all be firing at me.' (*Visor*, March 7 1974) This ironic view of the soldier as the innocent abroad even extended to self-deprecation. Not only are they allowed to show fear, as when two squaddies hold hands to comfort each other during a thunderstorm near the border, but they are often outwitted by the locals, though never by the Provisional IRA. A particularly favourite theme is the ability of local inhabitants to see through the cover of soldiers on secret surveillance, as when a whistling milkman leaves two bottles of milk outside an army undercover stakeout house: 'I think our cover's been blown', one pair of eyes inside the house comments to another (*Visor*, July 1974). The frequency with which the incompetent intelligence officer appears suggests that the soldier on the ground was less than impressed by his efforts.

He was equally unimpressed by the inhabitants of the benighted province in which he found himself, but the army cartoonists' images of the enemy were perhaps less jaundiced than one might expect. It is true that the popular Irish joke, which caricatures the Irishman as contradictory, stupid and most of all inferior, left its mark. The winner of the January 1976 *Visor* cartoon competition, for example, featured an imbecilic Irishman setting his alarm clock (with dynamite tubes attached) for seven o'clock to ensure that he would wake up in time to plant it. It may be significant however that this particular thick Irishman was clearly a terrorist going about his evil business.

While occasional cartoonists depicted the Irish in general as stupid, this was a relatively rare theme. By and large the stupidity of the Paddy was manifested only when he was planting bombs and land-mines. It may be, of course, that some soldiers believed all the Irish to revel in such activities. If not, there is an interesting and careful distinction between the cartoon terrorist and the cartoon Irishman.

So the army cartoonists from Northern Ireland act out the relationships between soldiers and gunmen within a context of bombs and bullets. Astonishingly, none are killed. In the 500-odd cartoons drawn by soldiers and published in *Visor*, not a single person from the ranks of either the army or

Terrorists or Freedom Fighters?

Heath/*Spectator*

'What d'you mean, we can keep him? We want fifteen prisoners.'

Mahood/*Punch*

"Jasus Sean! You can't go out to murder people dressed like that!"

Somewhere in the recesses of the media's folk memory of Irish violence lay the image of the Irish Republican Army. So closely linked were the two in the popular imagination that the IRA began to invade cartoons even before the Provisionals were formed in 1970. Most commentators agree that the IRA was a minor and ineffective force during these early years of the Troubles.

To fix the image of the newcomers, cartoonists simply picked it up where it had been left at the time of partition in 1921. Trench coats, slouch hats and Tommy guns were dusted off and called into service again, at least until new cues could be established. In case a new readership was unfamiliar with the image, armbands or badges helpfully inscribed 'IRA' were sometimes added. The transformation of this outmoded stereotype was gradual and

somewhat confusing. Black berets and dark glasses appeared, and even the trench coats eventually gave way to combat jackets. The confused image was turned to advantage by Mahood, who contrasted ancient and modern paramilitary modes, and by Martyn Turner, who pointed

the republicans has been killed. Bricks hit their heads, clothes are blown off in bomb explosions, soldiers are run down incessantly by civilians failing to halt at check barriers. But the conventions of cartoons, which permit Tom to squash, mangle, pummel, slice and otherwise abuse Jerry, come to the rescue, and the realities of death and mutilations which were faced daily by the soldiers are carefully excluded from their cartoons. This construction of an escapist cartoon world is clearly an attempt to relieve the tensions and fears of soldiers in Northern Ireland, so the ruined houses and the hostile crowds, the bombs and the guns are represented, but only as local colour, to provide a backcloth for the game played by the soldiers and their enemies.

Martyn Turner/*Fortnight*

PORTRAIT OF A TERRORIST

Cookson/*Punch*

"…and when you've been in the service six months you're promoted to the heavy horn-rimmed kind."

Cookson/*Punch*

"…above and beyond the call of duty…losing a lens in a skirmish in Kilburn…"

out that paramilitary prisoners in fact conformed to a disturbingly normal and alarmingly young pattern.

The dark glasses adopted primarily by loyalist groups became a favourite subject. In his series of cartoons on the theme in *Punch*, however, Cookson provided no

evidence as to whether his rather natty bespectacled paramilitaries were loyalist or republican. In fact most cartoonists were inclined to lump together not only all the different loyalist groups, and all the republican groups, but all paramilitaries.

Indeed Trog went out of his way to demonstrate that the Official and Provisional IRA were merely two bloody arms attached to the same body.

What motivated the gunmen? Some cartoonists suggested that they were driven by historical forces to court martyrdom; others like Friers supported the Godfather hypothesis—that the IRA leaders were cynical profiteers, like Mafia bosses; the predominant view, however, was that the only possible explanation lay

Nowhere is this better illustrated than in the adventures of Seamus, the IRA youth created by the soldier cartoonist Carr, and featured in *Visor's* regular strip cartoon (*see* Carr, N. D.). Seamus and the cheerful soldiers who commiserate with him as, each week, his plans to kill them go awry, inhabit a world which is entirely incredible. He may be hurt, but it is inconceivable that he could be killed; the soldiers smile cheerfully as they drive in open armoured cars over Seamus' land-mines, which are never properly connected. Seamus is not evil or simian, like Tenniel's Victorian Irishman. He is a buffoon, rather a likeable incompetent whose eternal function in life is to fall victim of his own bombs and the soldiers' condescension. But under-

Trog/*Punch*

A LICK AND A PROMISE

Barry Fantoni/*Listener*

'I know it breaks the heart, Liam, but we can't claim this one.'

in an inherent brutishness, or stupidity, or instability. Fantoni's two IRA men, still sartorially and ideologically entrenched, were almost a synopsis of earlier Irish caricatures, representing respectively brutality and imbecility.

neath the soldier's easy superiority and Seamus' continual search for nemesis is an even more unexpected relationship—a camaraderie between the two sides which acknowledges that they are both partners in the same *danse macabre*. There is no fear or dislike in the relationship, but an affection which is illustrated by *Visor's* Christmas cartoon of 1976, showing Carr in battle dress and Seamus, his creation, in his familiar young thug garb, faces wreathed in smiles and arms around each other.

This is not to say that all the cartoons drawn by soldiers are consistent with this analysis. On occasions a caustic note appears, made striking by its rarity. Virtually the only expression of frustration by soldiers about the restraints on

The same attributes ranked high in the *Loyalist News* strip cartoon 'Bill and Ben, the IRA men', who were treated with contempt and scorn. Seamus, their equivalent in the army newspaper *Visor* on the other hand, was so ineffectual that his intended military victims offer him kindly advice when his rocket launchers have backfired and his bombs failed to explode—rockets and bombs which were designed to kill them.

their activities was the sarcastic comment from a besieged squaddie over the phone to his officer: 'Main gate here requesting permission to shout "Bang"' (*Visor*, June 13 1974). There are also times when their views of the IRA are less tolerant than Carr's. Even on these occasions, however, the blame is laid at the feet of the leaders. 'At present almost 1,000 people are in the process of passing through the courts on charges involving terrorist activities', *Visor* commented in a front page story of September 26 1974. 'Many are juveniles conned into committing serious crimes by evil 'Fagins' who are not prepared to run the risk of being caught themselves.' An accompanying cartoon shows the IRA leaders living in comfort, far removed from danger. This godfather

Anti-IRA cartoons are to be expected from loyalist cartoonists. More interesting, however, is the official UDA cartoon which represents its political wing as a force for restraint rather than aggression.

Ulster Defence Association

Republican cartoonists rarely included the IRA in their drawings, preferring attacking their enemies to eulogising their heroes. Flags and other symbols took their place. There is a clear echo of Second World War propaganda posters in Oisin's 'The Informers', which is repeated in many other cartoons unsympathetic to Britain.

THE INFORMERS

Oisin/*Andersonstown News*

syndrome, which sees the conflict as a sort of extreme crime wave with young stupid louts manipulated by the godfathers of crime to line their own pockets, is a major theme of the army's view of Northern Ireland's violence.

So the cartoon world created by soldiers is inhabited variously by long-suffering smiling soldiers, stupid officers, randy housewives, Irishmen in the process of self-destruct, soldiers joining in Irish dances and Orange parades, discomfited soldiers and embarrassed soldiers. But the theme which carries the most heartfelt conviction is the wish to be out of it all. 'Goodbye to Ulster' and 'England or bust', are the captions accompanying many cartoons, as different regiments marked the end of their spell in Northern Ireland with drawings of drunken, singing, rejoicing—but most of all departing—soldiers leaving Ulster's shores.

Republicans

The combination of cheap offset litho printing and an intense political crisis produced a plethora of underground publications in Northern Ireland during the 1970s. All the major loyalist and republican organisations quickly saw the importance of producing their own newspapers or magazines, although these varied greatly in sophistication. Publication dates were regarded as less than sacrosanct and many only lasted for a few issues, to re-emerge later under another name. There elusiveness helped to ensure their immunity from legal action. One result of this is that the loyalist and republican newspapers accurately represent the most extreme and frank political views in the province, unadulterated by fear of censors or courts.

The most sophisticated of these publications are the *Republican News*, *An Phoblacht* and the *United Irishmen*. The greater polish of the republican newspapers over those published by loyalist organisations arises partly from their larger readership and income and partly from their concern to influence Irish–American as well as Irish republicans. The *Republican News*, for example, announced its price in cents as well as pence, and is fond of reproducing cartoons sympathetic to the republican cause from European and American publications.

The popularity of cartoons in the republican newspapers is not difficult to appreciate. A major function of the magazines is to bolster morale among a constituency of sympathisers, rather than to convert unaligned readers. By the very nature of the underground political press, there are very few un-committed readers. Cartoons are an ideal vehicle for crystallizing the messages which need to be transmitted to the faithful: the British, the Loyalists and the liberals in our own ranks are our enemies; we are winning but must persevere; informers will be killed, etc. So popular were the cartoons which appeared in the *Republican News* and later *An Phoblacht*, that, for a short period, they inspired the publication of a number of political comics, published under the name *Resistance Comix* (10 issues), and *People's Comix* (2 issues). These comics were soon dominated by one of the most interesting cartoonists to emerge from the Northern Irish conflict, Cormac, whose peculiar and effective use of comic strips is the only important cartooning innovation during the period. A selection of these cartoons and others which appeared in the British weekly *Socialist Challenge* was published in 1982 (Cormac 1982).

Cormac views the gloomy and violent streets of Belfast with a philosophical despair and cynical wit, and he peoples them with a caste which dances to his tune. The *dramatis personae* include the increasingly paranoid Paddy O'Looney, founder of the Irish section of the Sixth Intergalactic Revolutionary Movement, an anarchist who develops his theories in the Arm Alite bar: 'He is dedicated to the defeat of imperialism! He is dedicated to the smashing of capitalism! He is dedicated to the overthrow of the bourgeoisie of a brave new world! But mainly he is dedicated to having another pint of stout' (*Resistance Comix*, 2). Tommy the Tout* specializes in supplying useless information to the army—as when he informed the police through the confidential telephone about an SAS man killed in South Armagh, 'I think the Provos did it'—and being blown up in a variety of gruesome ways for this major crime of informing. Following readers' compaints about the absence of female characters, Cormac supplied Paddy O'Looney with a colleague, Red Biddy, the revolutionary feminist and scourge of Irish male chauvinism. There is a host of minor characters too, like The Brigadier who represents the stupidity of the British Officer class, Berty the Brit and Rick O'Shea, the Irish mystic.

Another character from *Resistance Comix*, although not drawn by Cormac, was featured in 'Seamus O'Ther and his boring adventures'. Seamus represented the common man, the innocent victim of the troubles, and his main preoccupations are 'going for a pint or sitting in the armchair thinking about going for a pint' (*Resistance Comix*, 3). This harmless enough ambition is constantly thwarted by soldiers, who harass, search and beat him. His support for the Provos continues throughout his bewilderment at this conduct, and he effortlessly gets the better of the soldiers.

* Tout is defined by Cormac as 'an informer—a class of person remarkable for their short life expectancy'. (*Resistance Comix*, 5)

The stage for these characters and adventures are the dull streets of Belfast and the troubles are viewed firmly in this context. 'Why this endless obsession with politics?' Cormac asks. 'Because, without the troubles, Belfast would be incredibly boring'. The few members of Paddy O'Looney's revolutionary group also find relief in a fatalist escapism and adopt the aphorism, 'Reality is a nice place for a holiday... but we wouldn't like to live there' (*Resistance Comix*, 3). Frequently the cartoonist Cormac features as a character in his own cartoons, usually as a mild alcoholic running out of ideas, losing arguments with his animated pen, which berates and lectures him about the poor quality of his drawings, his bad taste and the pointlessness of it all. Cormac sums up the constant theme of these dialogues thus: 'In Castlereagh barracks is torture, in H Block is pain, disease and misery... and here I sit listening to my pen spouting truisms... What does it all mean?' (*Resistance Comix*, 10).

The cartoons of Cormac which were printed in the comics and those produced in the *Republican News* and *An Phoblacht* attack different targets, although some were printed in both publications. In the *Peoples' Comix* there is a strong emphasis on socialist as well as republican ideals, and Cormac's most biting invective is reserved for a relatively innocuous target, the small group of liberal intellectuals who support the Provisionals, but who are not prepared to join in the fighting. Not surprisingly the Arm Alite bar is the venue where these 'public house anarchists, Guinness republicans, armchair revolutionaries, pseudo-socialists gather to slay the capitalists with words' (*Resistance Comix*, 8). In the *Republican News* and *An Phoblacht*, on the other hand, the targets for the cartoonists are the traditional enemies of Irish republicanism. This is clearly related to the function of *An Phoblacht* and the other papers sympathetic to the Provisional IRA. By their nature, which is to reinforce morale and to encourage solidarity, they are didactic and aggressive, and concentrate their venom on the enemies of the republican movement. Cormac and the other cartoonists have a clear role in this respect and the method of characterising the opponents is often crude and lacking in sublety.

There is no doubt about who are these main enemies of republicanism. Top of the list is Britain and the British army, and soldiers are the most frequent subjects in republican cartoon strips. The stereotyping is less than subtle. Soldiers are drawn as pigs and as stupid pawns of a privileged officer class. The officers are also strongly stereotyped and Cormac's six-part strip on the life of Captain Nervewreck—a reference to the career of Captain Nairac, a real British intelligence officer who was murdered in 1973—aroused some controversy when it was printed. Nervewreck's aristocratic background is described, his contemplating the church as a career—'C of E of course! none of that low-clas presbyterian rubbish'—and his eventual army career which ends in South Armagh. In what he considers a successful mimicing of a Belfast accent, Nervewreck is given a line of dialogue somewhere between Harry Lauder Scots and Barry Fitzgerald's brogue, with an occasional intervention by Ian Carmichael—'Hoots, mon, would you ever be giving me a pint of bitter, begorrah, the noo? And where would you be thinking I was from, old man—I mean, Bejapers, och aye?' The last frame of the last cartoon shows him being invited outside a bar, presumably to his execution (*Repub-*

Soldiers of the Queen

AND THEN MY DAD SAID "WHY DON'T YOU JOIN THE ARMY AND STOP STANDING AROUND ON STREET CORNERS"

Nicale/*Visor*

By far the largest single category of cartoons about Northern Ireland, from all sources, concerned the British army. Many of these were drawn by soldier-cartoonists and printed in *Visor*, the army's weekly newspaper in Northern Ireland. They present a composite picture of innocent squaddies surrounded by hostile Irish rioters, and reacting with tact and good humour. Their lack of ideological involvement in the conflict even allowed soldiers to show themselves as the butt of their own cartoons, scared or outwitted in a way which republican cartoonists never represent the IRA. The army cartoonist Carr even represented the friendly bonhomie between himself and his IRA character Seamus in his 1976 Christmas cartoon. But the favourite theme was the prospect of leave, and a succession of cartoons bade a heartfelt goodbye to Ulster as different regiments returned to Britain or were transferred to Germany.

lican News, February 11–March 3 1978).

Irish cartoonists like Cormac and Oisin were not the only ones to represent these themes. It is the British army presence more than any other which has made Northern Ireland a subject of interest throughout the world. The republican press was particularly fond of republishing cartoons from overseas publications which attacked the army. Pete Wagner, an American cartoonist, has had many cartoons republished in the Republican News, almost all attacking Britain and the British army, as did Steve Smith of the *British Socialist Worker*. The socialist press in Europe was also a rich source for anti-British cartoons, and many were reprinted. Not only did such

Carr/*Visor*

Visor

'Well it could be the Officials firing at Provos or the IRA firing at the Prots or the UDA firing at the Officials or the UVF firing at the Cats—on the other hand they could all be firing at me'?

cartoons reinforce the repubican opposition to the British army, but they also demonstrated that this view was shared by individuals and organisations in other countries.

Apart from the army, the targets of republican cartoonists were quite localised. Perhaps surprisingly the Ulster loyalists, despite their occasional appearance as assassins, bigots, and backwoodsmen and a short-lived strip cartoon of Ian Paisley as Superprod, were not a major preoccupation of republican cartoonists. It is noticeable, however, that they are regarded as synomymous with the Royal Ulster Constabulary, and some cartoonists invariably draw loyalist politicians, paramilitaries and the police complete with

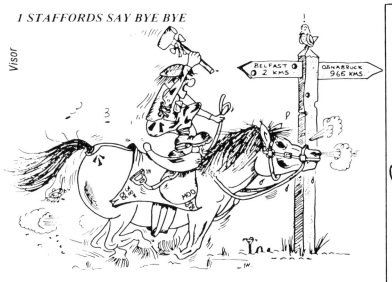

1 STAFFORDS SAY BYE BYE

Visor

Mahood/*Punch*

"The funny thing is we didn't even know that bigots celebrated Christmas."

Some of the same themes were echoed by many British cartoonists. While there were few overtly propagandist cartoons supporting the army, the dominant expression was one of sympathy. Soldiers were regarded as professionals carrying out a dirty and unwelcome job, and doing it well. Mahood's cartoons briefing soldiers who had been invited to join local families for Christmas in 1969 were really about the culture shock awaiting decent squaddies when they came into contact with a new and bigoted species. When criticism was expressed, it was directed towards the politicians whose coals were being pulled out of the fire by the army.

Orange regalia and sashes. A much more popular target than the loyalists were those political parties and organisations which sought their support mainly or partly from the same Catholic community as the Provisionals did. The Social Democratic and Labour Party (SDLP) and the Peace People are the objects of the most bitter attacks and their leaders caricatured as insincere profiteers. Gerry Fitt, then leader of the SDLP, appeared as a shifty-eyed, cigarette-smoking con-man in happy alliance with the unionist parties—a reference to the short-lived power-sharing Executive when three parties formed a government in 1974. The Official IRA and, later, the Republican clubs and the Workers' Party, are also viewed as competitors for Catholic

'THE ARMY IS WINNING THE WAR IN NORTHERN IRELAND'

Horner/New Statesman

Rab/Loyalist News

Horner in the *New Statesman* came as close to attacking the army as any major British cartoonist. He suspected that the army was being manipulated by the Ulster Unionists for their own ends, and went on to suggest that army press releases forecasting imminent victory should only be swallowed with a large grain of salt.

More hostile views were expressed, not only by overseas cartoonists, but by all paramilitary groupings. Attacks by loyalist cartoonists on the Paratroop regiment were unequalled for venom, and Cormac of the *Republican News* viewed the British army as a large number of vicious louts led by a small number of cretinous officers. His solution to the problem was simple and graphic.

support, and are characterized as ineffective and opportunist. The perceived insignificance of the middle ground in Ulster politics is demonstrated by the fact that the Northern Ireland Labour Party has not featured in any republican cartoons, and the leaders of the Alliance Party, which also sought cross-sectarian support, only appeared infrequently and as forlorn ineffective figures on the periphery of important events.

For all this clarity and singularity of their objectives, republican cartoonists have some difficulty in depicting the fighting itself and the men of the Provisional IRA whom they support. Unlike the cartoons produced by British soldiers, republican cartoons are graphic in their depiction of injuries and

Cormac/*Republican News*

Scarfe/*Sunday Times*

death. Heads are cracked like egg-shells, blood flows, limbs are shattered and men die. An illustration in *Resistance Comix* shows a shattered head, with eyes, ears and brains flying, and is accompanied by the caption, 'Serious self-defence requires pretty heavy artillery. The defence of the Catholic ghettoes needs more than karate experts' (*Resistance Comix*, 2). Indeed, men and women die in republican cartoons, not to shock readers into opposing violence, but to underline the justification for the Provisionals' use of violence. The cartoons which represent the Provisionals themselves—and there are surprisingly few of these—are often clichéd and wooden. Frivolity of

THE PROFESSIONALS

Oisin/*Andersonstown News*

The differences in attitude towards the army presence is encapsulated in two cartoons by Scarfe and Oisin. Both adopted as their theme the army recruitment slogan 'Join the Professionals'. However Scarfe's cartoon is about the use of the army by the government as a jack of all trades for dirty and unpopular jobs; there is no criticism of the soldiers. Oisin's view, on the other hand, was that Ireland was the latest in a shameful chronicle of British involvement in assassinations and deaths as her empire crumbled around her.

speech or demeanour is shunned, and the republican soldier almost invariably appears as a demigod, young, clear-eyed and visionary with eyes fixed firmly on the horizon. There is no example of a republican cartoon depicting a Provisional soldier outwitted, as frequently happens British soldiers in their cartoons. It seems likely that the difference relates to their relative commitments to the struggle.

The ineffectuality of the provisional republicans in depicting the violence and their combatants is even more marked in the cartoons published in the other anti-unionist, socialist magazines—the *Irish Trotskyite*, the *Irish Worker* and others. Their problem is to attack the establishment without supporting the Provisionals, who were for most of the decade the only anti-unionist group actively involved in violence. The most frequent way of overcoming this political difficulty is to concentrate on political events, a minor theme among Provisional cartoonists who have sharper axes to grind, and on general attacks on British army atrocities. The impression gained is one of cartoonists carefully treading a narrow path, which is essentially a contradiction in terms. It is fair to add that the resulting ineffectiveness of the cartoons published in these other anti-Unionist papers, is partly due to their lacking a cartoonist of Cormac's ability.

Loyalists

The loyalist paramilitary news-sheets—if anything more numerous than the republican ones—are discernably different in tone and appearance. In general they are shorter, less sophisticated in layout, printed or duplicated on cheaper paper and less ambitious in their projected readership. Their aspirations and content are proudly provincial, and strongly reinforce the territorial integrity of loyalist areas against republican encroachments. However, they share with the republican papers a fondness for cartoons.

The effectiveness of the loyalist cartoons is somewhat impaired by both the poor quality of their reproduction and by a shortage of good cartoonists. In general they are crudely drawn, roughly lettered and lacking sublety. A favourite device is to pirate cartoons from the English popular daily newspapers, add on a caption with some local theme and convert the cartoon characters into their republican opponents—Bernadette Devlin, Fat Pat the IRA rat (Paddy Devlin), pregnant nuns, effeminate, drunk priests and large Catholic families. The only significant loyalist cartoonist to emerge has been Rab, inventor of the strip cartoon 'Bill and Ben the IRA men', whose general stupidity and activities bear a marked resemblance to Carr's Seamus strip in

Visor, the army weekly. Rab was the cartoonist who drew the poster of two republicans lynched and hanging from lampposts. 'Support the IRA' was its slogan.

The single-mindness of the loyalist attacks on Catholics and republicans—regarded as synonymous terms—provides an interesting contrast to the variety of targets attacked by republican cartoonists. The republicans regard their conflict as a war of liberation against an external enemy and its army of occupation, and they are preoccupied with cartoons featuring the British army; their treatment of other targets—Nationalist politicians and loyalist paramilitaries in the main—is rooted in the consequent need for Catholic anti-unionist cohesion against this threat. To the Loyalists their struggle is for the survival of Ulster against the enemy within the province, republicans, fenians, papists, who are attempting to overthrow it by bombs and bullets. These single-minded attacks are hammered home. 'Let's laugh at our enemies' (*Orange Cross*, 65) and 'Taking the mickey' (*Loyalist News*, January 13 1973)—Mickey is a term used in Northern Ireland to denote Catholics—are collections of cartoons in the *Loyalist News* which reveal an obsession with priests, nuns and the confessional but are often quite benevolent. A more venomous note appears when the cartoonists detect concessions to Roman Catholics. The theme of threatened Protestant privileges is a major one not only for cartoonists but running throughout the loyalist press. Republicans have better prison conditions, softer jail sentences, get better jobs and generally are pampered in a way which might cause some raised eyebrows among the readers of the *Republican News*. It is only rarely, however, that the level of invective has the paranoid racist tones of the cover of Clifford Smyth's pamphlet entitled *Rome—our enemy*, which the *Loyalist News* reprinted as a cartoon. A sinister pope, fingers dripping blood over an outline map of Ulster, is reminiscent of the European anti-semitic cartoons of the nineteenth century (Smyth 1973).

Loyalist views towards the British army in Ulster were rather ambivalent. The traditional fierce attachment to Britain dictated that it was their army, and furthermore one which was increasingly involved in direct conflict with the Provisional IRA. During 1972 and 1973, however, the loyalist Ulster Defence Association become active on the streets and inevitably came into conflict with the army. The reaction was one of shock, almost effrontery. The cartoonists adapted to this dilemma by expressing general sympathy towards the army, but selectively attacking particular regiments at particular times. Army squaddies were shown admiring the courage and skill of the UDA—'Thank God this lot are for us—I'd hate them to be against us' (*Loyalist News*,

August 11 1973)—and they clearly belonged to the same side. The paratroop regiment was another matter. 'Paranoia, Parasite, Paralysed, Paralytic', accompanied four unflattering cartoons of soldiers in the regiment (*Loyalist News*, April 27 1974). Indeed dislike of the paratroopers is a rare case where the loyalist and republican cartoonists vie with each other in invective. The mock army recruiting poster printed in the *Loyalist News* in 1972 would have been appreciated by the readers of the *Republican News*: 'Can you shoot unarmed men or beat girls with your rifle? Then be a Para' (*Loyalist News*, April 20 1974).

Not all the loyalist cartoons are so bitter. The violence also breeds its own wry humour, like Rab's drawings of a street-corner hold-up. One sinister individual addresses his victim. 'Spare a few bob for a man with nothing in his pocket but a loaded '45, sir'.

The Views of the Combatants

In some respects there are remarkable similarities between many of the republican and loyalist cartoons and those published in *Visor*. The attraction of particular themes—the enemy falling victim to their own bombs, guns and other war paraphernalia, army under-cover operations which are invariably detected, etc.—cuts across other differences. There is also a curious tendency among all three interests to depict their enemies as physically small and significant, which may reveal latent ethnic stereotyping. Oisin in the *Andersonstown News* and Cormac draw British politicians like Roy Mason and Scottish soldiers as subnormal midgets, just as some soldier–cartoonists like to represent the IRA.

It is in their differences, however, that the cartoons of the three protagonists are most revealing about the parties themselves and about the nature of their aspirations and fears. British army cartoonists, for example, perceive themselves as detached professionals, surveying the Northern Irish scene with a gaze somewhere between stoicism and a mildly amused condescension. They clearly operate in an active service area fraught with real danger, but it is an area which, apart from the violence itself, has little to distinguish it from any other western society. References to local events or personalities are rare: Ian Paisley occasionally features in army cartoons, but almost invariably as a stereotype for a certain extravagant style and eccentric attitudes; Enoch Powell is another favourite subject for soldier–cartoonists, usually with his face blacked for undercover patrols, but he is clearly seen as a British personality rather than as the member of parliament for South Down. In general, on the few occasions when they stray into local comment, the views expressed are often naive or ignorant.

Curiously enough, police cartoonists showed a similar reluctance to deal with the local conflict in Northern Ireland, and with the violence which threatened many of their lives. *Police Beat*, a monthly magazine produced by the Police Federation in Northern Ireland since 1979, uses a large number of cartoons, many by a skilled cartoonist called Graham Patterson. Almost without exception, their themes are about constabulary rather than paramilitary duties, and there is no suggestion that the jokes are located in Northern Ireland. A rare exception is the sardonic humour of a featured poster cartoon in 1980: as a prisoner in the dock disclaims, 'Actually, I was well treated in Castlereagh' (that is, the interrogation barracks which had attracted much criticism), everyone in the court—defence, prosecution, press, court officials and resident magistrate—fall about in incredulous mirth (*Police Beat*, 2, 3, 1980).

Provisional republican cartoons and the newspapers in which they appear both reveal concerns and nuances within Northern Irish republicanism which contradict the image of a monolithic movement sometimes presented by commentators. At different times they are aggressive and defensive, extrovert and parochial, and they reserve their strongest abuse for other groups within the broadly nationalist spectrum—the Official IRA, the Social Democratic and Labour party and other radical anti-Unionist groups. Their concern with presenting their fighting men as pure, highly motivated and ideologically sophisticated makes it impossible to acknowledge any signs of weakness and very few signs of good humour. Almost without exception, the cartoons which deal with the actual fighting cross the narrow boundary between the humorous cartoon and the propaganda poster; the possibility of a camaraderie between fighting men on different sides, which is a theme in some army cartoons, is therefore unthinkable. These apparent differences in emphasis can mainly be explained by the need of the Provisionals to address two different interests, their supporters within Northern Ireland and their sympathisers outside it. In the former case the main emphases are on the danger of fragmenting republican unity and the threat of internal erosion; in the latter, the focus is on the integrity of both the problem and its solution, both of which are rooted in the presence of Britain and its army on Irish soil.

Solidarity is also a major theme in loyalist cartoons, but the treatment is much more introverted. Although most of the rival loyalist paramilitary organisations have their own newspapers, there are few public signs of disagreement or feuding between them. Attention is focused on the agreed enemy, the republican rebels, and side swipes at secondary targets like the Parachute regiment are only occasional. It is accepted without question that interests outside Northern Ireland are usually hostile to loyalist interests, so the need to consider such external forces is non-existent. As a consequence, most of the cartoons lack sophistication and are characterised by a casual crudity, in both the scatological and artistic senses of the word. The characters who appear in them are recognisably working people, and lack the classical heroism of their equivalents in republican newspapers.

So an important key to the differences between republican, loyalist and army cartoons is how each group perceives its constituency. *Visor*, for example, is not intended for readers outside the troops stationed in Northern Ireland, and has some of the flavour of a house journal or school magazine—parochial, gossipy and unselfconscious; the fact that they are stationed in Northern Ireland is almost incidental. A similar parochialism pervades loyalist cartoons and newspapers, which also have a closed and familiar constituency, but their flavour is distinctively Northern Irish. Indeed they are almost exclusively concerned with internal Northern Irish affairs, and the root of the problem is clearly identified as the republican enemy within. The republicans, on the other hand, are the only actors concerned with an external as well as an internal constituency, and the only ones who define the problem as an external one, the presence of Britain. So, while their cartoons share with loyalists the function of rallying the faithful and encouraging morale and cohesion among them, they have also a propaganda role by reminding overseas supporters that there are international elements to the violence, and that international pressure and support are significant factors in maintaining the struggle. Hence the need for more sophisticated presentation, and cartoons which focus on the theme of British oppression and imperialism.

As Others See It: 5
The View from Abroad

Do you want to know what posterity will say? Find out what contemporary foreigners say.

H. S. Constable

THE mountain of cartoons printed throughout the world which must be sifted to find a few grains on the Irish conflict is enough to test the industry of even the most energetic polyglot. In the United States alone, every city of even moderate size has at least one daily newspaper, while cartoons also feature in hundreds of magazines and periodicals. As a result, it is difficult to proceed from general observations to authoritative analysis. It is possible, because of their more limited outlets, to study quite thoroughly the output of British, Irish and paramilitary cartoonists; this has been the object in the other chapters of this book. No such claim is made for this chapter. Its purpose is to provide a taste of how some cartoonists from abroad have viewed the conflict, and its justification is the conclusion, even on preliminary evidence, that the view so often contrasts strongly with those provided in Ireland and Britain. The cartoons which will be discussed, which come from a wide variety of social and political settings, demonstrate the effects of distance on the cartoonist's approach, as well as the relationship between a country's political cartoons and its political system. It is not claimed that these conclusions are other than tentative.

The most consistent outside reaction to the conflict has come from the Soviet Union. To judge from *Pravda* and *Krokodil*, Soviet cartoonists' interest in Northern Ireland peaked in the periods following the Civil Rights campaign in 1969 and Internment in 1971. To N. Lisogorski, the political cartoonist whose work appeared in *Krokodil*, the weekly cartoon magazine, Northern Ireland was primarily regarded as an illustration of British duplicity and imperialism. In one of his favourite images John Bull aims at two targets on a wall, Racism in Rhodesia and Civil Rights in Northern Ireland, but the former is being attacked by a popgun and the latter with a machine-gun. This comparative approach was also popular with other Russian cartoonists (*Krokodil*, November 1969). In 1975, *Pravda* presented a British paratrooper with a machine-gun alongside two similarly armed soldiers from Chile and

South Africa in a common front of oppression, and a more obscure comparison between Northern Ireland and Guatemala featured in the same paper later in the year (March 16). As recently as 1981 the English-language *Moscow News* reverted to the theme of British bullying and oppression. A hand from Britain clamped a police helmet, unconvincingly covered with prison bars, over a map of Northern Ireland. 'Got it!' was the caption. These cartoons featuring the Northern Irish conflict are not exceptional in tone or approach within the context of the Soviet media. Political crises throughout the world—Panama, Vietnam, Rhodesia *et al.*—were chiefly regarded by Russian cartoonists as convenient vehicles for attacking their real targets,

Foreign Voices

'Northern Ireland is reported outside Britain as a colonial problem', wrote Jonathan Dimbleby in 1978. 'History has told us, and tells us, and will tell us, that Northern Ireland is our last colonial issue'. Such was the dominant view of Northern Ireland presented by Russian cartoonists in *Pravda* and *Krokodil* and, in a rare instance of international accord, by Wagner and some other North American cartoonists.

The European press too, and especially socialist cartoonists, did not disguise their pleasure at Britain's predicament in Northern Ireland. The spectrum of opinion ranged from Juhl's relatively benign comment on British incompetence to the

Pete Wagner/reprinted in *Republican News*

American imperialism and military dictatorships. By this measure Northern Ireland was a minor theme. *Pravda*, which publishes a considerable quantity of cartoons, only printed two featuring Northern Ireland between 1975 and 1979, both concerning British oppression. While Britain was regarded as a capitalist power, and therefore worth attacking, it was also regarded as a pale spectre of its imperial past, so not worth major attention. Hence Russian cartoons rarely referred to specific incidents in the province, but almost invariably placed it in a broader context of imperialism and in a comparative setting. Northern Ireland's role, alongside South Africa and Chile, was largely to make up the numbers.

Lissorgsky/*Krokodil*

It depends what he's aiming at.

Juhl/*Copenhagen PIB*

"Move on! Or I'll... er... I don't know what I'll do!"
DENMARK—Juhl *(Copenhagen PIB)*

Patrik/reprinted in *Resistance Comix*

French cartoonist Patrik, who presented Britain as a malign bully who had not only bitten off more than she could chew, but who ended up by being swallowed herself.

A similar scepticism about British motives in Northern Ireland was also evident among some North American cartoonists. The distrust extended to the British sources of news about the conflict, and is well demonstrated by these extracts from a mock quiz printed in December 1969 in the Canadian magazine, *Last Post:*

THE BIAS OF THE MEDIA

What is the question under survey to be known as?
The Irish Question.
In making this question meaningful to our many readers, what spectre may be

The Spanish cartoon, 'Arriba! Arriba!' also suggested that a rude shock awaited British imperialism.

Despite the almost universal criticism of British policy in Northern Ireland, active support for the IRA was largely confined to socialist cartoonists, who often regarded them as freedom fighters. Most of the prestigious American cartoonists, like Oliphant of the *Denver Post*, were openly hostile to the Provisionals and to their supporters in the United States.

'The followin' blast is brought to you by the lovin' donations of our loyal American cousins in the Irish Northern Aid Committee, may their names be blessed!'

referred to without fear of contradiction?
The spectre of religious hatred.
What part of this spectre's anatomy shall be singled out for special treatment?
Its ugly head.
In our second paragraph may we again mention religious hatred?
We may not.
What then may we substitute?
Sectarian strife.
To whom may this strife be ascribed?
To Extremist Elements on Both Sides.
What may we refer to the British troops in Ireland as trying to do?

Benson/*Arizona Republic*

Keep the peace.
Name several other characteristics (salient) and facts (basic, underlying) to be taken into consideration.

(a) alcohol (suggested format, 'The unfortunate Irish propensity for...')
(b) volatile Celtic exuberance (see files, French Canada, for sugg. format.)
(c) protestant fears (sugg. form. 'spokesmen voiced concern over...')

The Canadian media, perhaps because of their own connections with Britain, have also printed some of the most anti-British cartoons to appear in North America. Parker and Macpherson, in remarkably similar *Toronto Post* cartoons, represented a pipe-smoking Harold Wilson as Britannia, complete

Auth/*The Philadelphia Inquirer*

'I WAS AFRAID HE'D NEVER DIE...'

Austen/*Private Eye*

"Wanting to lose a bit of weight isn't a good enough reason for joining the IRA"

The popular view is that this was all changed by the H Block controversy and hunger strikes in 1980 and 1981, and that world opinion swung towards the IRA. Certainly for many cartoonists the two main themes were British political intransigence and the cynical willingness of IRA leaders to trade lives for publicity. After the death of Bobby Sands, however, opinion in the United States moved discernably towards the latter view. Cartoons by Steve Benson of the *Arizona Republic* and Tony Auth of the *Philadelphia Inquirer* showed a revulsion which was echoed in many overseas cartoons. This reaction is all the more marked when compared with the treatment of the issue in the British Press: here, although general interest was high, there were very few cartoons about H Blocks or hunger strikes. However, those which did appear in *Private Eye* showed no sympathy for the strikers.

with trident: one showed his Union Jack shield protecting a Protestant who is punching a Catholic urchin; the other cunningly converted Britannia's throne to a bath chair, being propelled by an urchin labelled 'Ulster' to the brink of anarchy. In the United States, a much tougher stance was taken by Pete Wagner of the *Minnesota Daily*, whose anti-British cartoons attracted the accolade of reproduction in the Provisionals' *Republican News*. The theme for Wagner was simply one of British imperialism and oppression. Irish blood dripped from the hands of a British soldier, evocatively uniformed in the style of the American war of Independence, in a 1975 cartoon. In others, Britain was rather obscurely presented as the barrier against Catholic–

Y. U. Kershina/*Pravda*

ЧИЛИ   ОЛЬСТЕР   ЮАР

"OH, OH, PADDY, NOW WE'VE GONE AND DONE IT!"

Wayne Stayskal (copyrighted, 1974, *Chicago Tribune*. Used with permission.)

There was a discernable relationship between cartoonists' approaches to subjects and their distance from it. Few cartoons about Ulster which appeared outside the British Isles reveal any detailed knowledge of events in the province. Instead Northern Ireland was commonly used as a convenient metaphor for such general social characteristics as terrorism, colonialism or bigotry. Soviet cartoonists, for example, were fond of presenting Northern Ireland alongside South Africa, Chile and Guatemala as oppressed victims of militarism, and Staygal of *Chicago Today* pictured Belfast as a frontier town where not even angels were safe from assassins. The effect offered little cause for rejoicing in the Northern Ireland Tourist Office.

Protestant accord in Northern Ireland. The most striking of these showed the warship of British imperialism ploughing a furrow between Catholic Ireland and Protestant Ireland.

However, this view was far from universal among North American cartoonists. Wayne Stayskal, editorial cartoonist of *Chicago Today*, found in the Northern Irish conflict an occasional pulpit for his Christianity; two armed IRA men survey an assassinated angel lying outside the Hotel Belfast: 'Oh, oh, Paddy... Now we're gone and done it' (*Chicago Today*, February 1 1974). Oliphant of the *Washington Star*, one of the most widely syndicated cartoonists in America, was also shocked by the apparent pointlessness of the fighting. He was one of many cartoonists to display its logical conclusion, a lone Irishman sitting on a tombstone and saying, 'Here I am, the last livin' person in Ireland, and I can't remember if I'm Catholic or Protestant'. For Oliphant the villain of the piece was the IRA and he drew one of the most outspoken cartoons of all, attacking American support for its activities: a bomb is tossed into Mooney's pub above the caption, 'The following blast is brought to you by the lovin' donations of our loyal American cousins in the Irish Northern Aid Committee, may their names be blessed' (*Denver Post*, December 23 1975). With some exceptions, however, American cartoonists generally treated the conflict as their Soviet counterparts did, demonstration of a universal malaise. For the Russians the malaise was imperialism; for many Americans it was a vague concern about violence and international terrorism.

Perhaps the single incident during the violence which attracted the greatest number of American cartoons about Northern Ireland was the IRA hunger strike campaign in 1980–81. It was popularly believed at the time that the accompanying propaganda war between the British government and the IRA about the H Blocks dispute and the strikes had resulted in an IRA victory. If this was so, it was not reflected in American cartoons. On the contrary, comments by such major American cartoonists as MacNelly, Auth and Benson were deeply critical of the IRA. Auth believed that the main rejoicing over the death of the hunger striker Bobby Sands came from the Provisionals; Benson contrasted the ceremonial surrounding Sands' funeral with the unpublicised burial of child victims of IRA violence; MacNelly showed hooded gunmen stealing a baby's bottle for use as a petrol bomb 'for the war effort'. Although there was also criticism by cartoonists of the British government in European and American publications sympathetic to Irish republicanism, the mainstream cartoonists had no doubts about who were the real villains.

Outside the USSR and North America, the reactions of cartoonists to Northern Ireland appear to be even more varied. Juhl of *Copenhagen PIB* depicted Harold Wilson as a harassed and incompetent policeman failing to direct the Belfast–Londonderry bus, with segregated seating and rioting passengers (September 1969). There was a clear holier-than-thou tone in the *Natal Mercury* cartoon on November 27 1969: a clean-cut South African rugby player stood surveying a furious Catholic–Protestant scrum, as an Ulster official says, 'Sorry, chum, this battlefield is already booked'. When the Australian cartoonist Robert McDougall drew six cartoons following a visit to Belfast in 1971, he found little to contribute which did not fit comfortably alongside the other Irish cartoons which had appeared in *Punch*.

The main exception to this low level of interest was among some European left-wing cartoonists. Their major theme was British oppression of the Irish, and a rather typical cartoon printed by the German *Solidaritatskomitee* represented the entire island, including the Irish Republic, as a concentration camp. The gilt on the gingerbread, however, was Britain's apparent inability to defeat the IRA. The French cartoonist Patrik, in a strip cartoon in 1978, showed a British soldier stepping into Ireland from England, being swallowed by its mouth—located in Belfast lough—chewed up and finally spat out as bones into the Irish sea (*Irlande Libre*, January 1978). More clever was the unsigned 1975 cartoon reprinted in the *Republican News* (January 25 1975). A large cat with a union jack coat is about to pounce on a mouse dressed with dark glasses and black beret, unaware that the mouse is about to detonate a bomb delicately sited under its tail. 'Arriba! Arriba!' was the caption.

So cartoons about Northern Ireland which have been printed overseas were greatly varied, but their approach was almost invariably conditioned by a common ignorance of the intricacies of the conflict. If cartoonists were unfamiliar with Ulster politics, or the infighting between conflicting loyalist and republican groups, they were more likely to regard Northern Ireland as an opportunity to make global observations about human behaviour. Imperialism, violence and self-determination comprised their major concerns. Similarly, in a geographical sense, they are more preoccupied with a major, if declining, world power than with an obscure Irish province. The Ulster cartoons were frequently not about Ulster at all, but about Britain, and the theme more often about the death throes of imperialism than about the effect of violence on a small community. Even when the cartoons focused on Northern Ireland rather than Britain, it was considered as an allegory for bigotry and mindless violence rather than as a subject in its own right. Thus Corky featured the IRA alongside a Cuban refugee and a Palestinian hyjacking a 'plane, although no 'plane had been hyjacked by Irish terrorists during the

Northern Irish crisis. More revealing, when the editor of the Australian newspaper *The Age* was asked if any Northern Irish cartoons had appeared in his publication since 1969 he was only able to recollect one example: drawn by Les Tanner in 1970, one clergyman is writing 'No Popery' on a wall, while another instructs him, '…Then sign it, Your Brother in Christ'. The cartoon is clearly about religious bigotry. The point is, however, that nowhere is suggested in the cartoon that the scene was taking place in Northern Ireland; the association was an unconscious one in the mind of the editor. By 1982 Northern Ireland had become a convenient shorthand metaphor for casual violence, religious bigotry or imperialist oppression to most overseas cartoonists.

Cartoonists in Conflict

Ask the cartoonist first, for he knows best.

W. H. Auden

THE cartoonist does not produce his drawings in a void. Indeed, the context in which he operates, whether defined as his nation or the newspaper for which he works, provides him with both themes and constraints. These are the subject of this chapter. It will examine national differences in the views of Northern Ireland presented by cartoonists, assess the ability of the cartoonist to depict his own views despite editorial constraints, and suggest that the cartoons on the Northern Irish conflict since 1969 have performed four main functions.

Changing Images

The effect of a cartoon is sudden, or not at all. Its purpose is to strip an issue to its bare essentials, and to deliver a single, effective interpretation of it. As the caricaturist selects the physical feature which distinguishes his target from all others, the political cartoonist tries to reduce each issue to its essential elements. Each cartoonist sees these differently. Consequently, when there is a high level of conformity in the treatment of certain issues, it is a matter for examination rather than acceptance.

The ways in which cartoonists have regarded Ireland have varied considerably over the last two centuries, and have continued to adjust to new developments during the 1970s. The frequency and intensity of cartoons, whether they appeared in Ireland, Britain or abroad, are closely connected to the level of violence and to the extent to which each country has been affected by it. In seventeenth century Britain, anti-Irish cartoons were common during the violent years of the 1640s, but diminished considerably for the following century and a half, until the 1798 rebellion revived British distaste for Irish rebels. The unpopularity which accompanied Irish immigration to both Britain and the United States from the 1840s is also strongly reflected in cartoons; on the other hand, the Stormont years, when minority grievances in Northern Ireland excited very little interest, were also ignored by cartoonists.

The attitude of Southern Irish cartoonists towards the North since 1969 demonstrates a similar unevenness, reflecting the extent to which Northern violence threatened the South at different times.

In all these instances the key factor was fear of Irish violence rather than concern for the problems of Ireland—or later Northern Ireland—and during each crisis the images were very consistent. The apish Irish thug of the mid-nineteenth century, for example, had lost its popularity by the turn of the century, and only appeared rarely during the 1970s. Indeed each period of violence produced its own stereotypes, and its own dynamic. By 1980 the rather benign image of the 1969 rioters had given way in English cartoons to an almost universal distaste for all things Irish, clearly reflecting more general changes in the way the issue was regarded. But the constant characteristics attributed to the Irish, regardless of changing fashions and conventions, were generally agreed—stupidity, unreliability and an inbred attraction to violence.

Distance and Disenchantment: The Cartoonist in his National Context

Of all the factors accounting for the different images of the conflict presented in cartoons, the nationality of the cartoonist is the most powerful. The all-party agreement on Northern Ireland, for example, has encouraged a high level of consensus among British cartoonists. In the Irish Republic, it would not be possible to estimate, on the basis of its political stance, in which magazine or newspaper any single cartoon had appeared. Outside the British Isles, there are clear differences in emphasis between socialist and capitalist countries, but general agreement among all that the issue is essentially to be viewed as a British problem, and treated as a metaphor for imperialism, or national liberation, or terrorism; in the United States, for example, there are no obvious disagreements on the issue between Republican and Democrat newspapers. Even in Northern Ireland's orthodox publications there is an evident liberal consensus. It is only in the cartoons which appear in the loyalist and republican newspapers that sharper political differences burst rudely to the fore. Otherwise, with minor exceptions, the main differences between cartoons are national rather than political. British cartoons, cartoons from the Irish Republic, American cartoons, Russian cartoons—all are distinguishable groups, and each has a high level of internal consistency. Although styles and treatments vary, the American cartoons are, above all else, distinctly American, and the British cartoons British. Most could have appeared in any newspaper of each country, regardless of its political affiliations.

The general effect of this variation is clear: the greater the distance between the cartoonist and Northern Ireland, the more uncomplicated the analysis and the broader the proposed solution. So, within the province itself, the orthodox cartoonists' awareness of the complexities often made it difficult to reach unqualified conclusions, except in their reactions to violence. In the United States and Europe, on the other hand, the analyses were rarely disturbed by such detailed knowledge; it was much easier to criticise the parties in conflict, or to propose bland and unworkable solutions.

The two main explanations for the strong distinctions between cartoonists from different settings are the level of their involvement with the issue, and the way in which they perceive their constituencies. This is demonstrated most clearly by the cartoons in military and paramilitary newspapers. British

The Media

Horner/*New Statesman*

THE MAN IN THE HOOD

The conduct of large-scale military operations within the United Kingdom created serious problems of news presentation, particularly for British commentators. Was it to be treated as an internal disturbance, and covered in the same way as a violent strike or a racial riot? Or was it in all but name a foreign war?

In Britain there was considerable pressure on the media to act as they had done during the Second World War. Interviews with the IRA and their supporters aroused public fury, and twenty-eight television programmes on Northern Ireland were banned, censored or delayed between 1970 and 1978. The predominant concern was that the media would provide a platform for terrorists, and undermine the work of the army. As Jay Blumler pointed out, 'the critics are asking only one question about Ulster coverage: not if it is accurate, if it deals with the important developments, if it is clarifying, or even if it is fair, but simply—is it demoralising?'

army cartoonists represent the soldiers as detached professionals carrying out a distasteful job; the political issue does not interest them very much. Cartoonists in Provisional newspapers, on the other hand, express a much greater commitment to national liberation and anti-colonialist struggles; their constituency is clear, and their cartoons have a strong polemical and propagandist function. In contrast to both of these, cartoons from Britain and the Irish Republic often reveal fundamental contradictions. Both countries officially claim that Northern Ireland is an integral part of their concept of nationality, but these claims are not echoed by their cartoonists. Thus, although Northern Ireland is part of the United Kingdom, one has only to contrast the

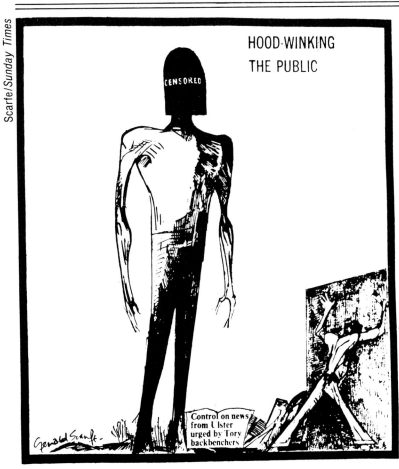

Scarfe/Sunday Times

HOOD-WINKING
THE PUBLIC

CENSORED

Control on news from Ulster urged by Tory backbenchers

Gerald Scarfe

Information on Ireland

THIS IS THE
NINE O'CLOCK
NEWS

It was left to people in the media themselves to express concern about the accuracy of news coverage on the conflict. Both Horner and Scarfe pointed to the parallel between the illegal hooding of prisoners during interrogation and hooding the press which might seek to report it.

different treatment of IRA bombs in Birmingham and Belfast to demonstrate its marginality to most British cartoonists. Similarly, although cartoons from the Irish Republic often reflect its territorial claim to Northern Ireland, real concern is expressed only when there appears to be danger of the violence spilling over the border.

It is in the British cartoons that the most serious, and the most illuminating, dilemmas are evident. The arrival of the British army on the streets of Belfast in 1969 complicated what had been a relatively clear-cut issue. Before that time the dispute had been regarded as an internal riot, rather like the later race riots in Toxteth, though more peripheral. This model provided cartoon-

Information on Ireland

Cormac/Republican News

There was little sympathy for the predicament of the press among republican cartoonists, and Cormac in the *Republican News* constantly depicted the media as little more than mouthpieces for British propaganda.

The cartoon which won the *New Statesman* cartoon competition in 1973 *Administering the Last Rites, Ulster* emphasised a new complication in assessing the balance between news reporting and propaganda.

For the first time the Northern Irish conflict was taking place under the constant attention of the world's press and television, as Blotski pointed out. In such circumstances the media themselves become part of the issue they are reporting, and their approval the object of the combatants.

ists with options: they could focus on the danger to life and property, on the social and economic distress which must lie behind them, on police brutality, or on the grievances of the rioters. The violence in Northern Ireland was less clear cut. On the one hand, it had the appearance of a riot, internal to the United Kingdom; on the other, it increasingly resembled a war: the army was not usually involved in riot control; the casualty rate rose alarmingly; there was an external dimension, with the underlying demand for Irish unification; and, whatever the constitutional arrangements, Northern Ireland was emotionally regarded by many British people as foreign and expendable. The consequences of this dilemma for cartoonists, and for the British

Sam Thompson/*New Statesman*

Administering the
Last Rites, Ulster

media in general were very serious. If the violence in Northern Ireland was to be regarded as a war, their options were much more limited. Criticism of official policy, or of army behaviour, might be seen as giving support to the enemy, and smack of treason. Between 1969 and 1975, the view presented of Northern Ireland by British cartoonists made this transition from riot to war.

As a result, British cartoonists tended to avoid those aspects of the Ulster issue which would normally emphasise the differences between the political left and right: the suspension of due legal process, such as the introduction of Internment in 1971 and the Diplock non-jury trials from 1975, were not popular subjects. Neither was criticism of the army. Even when official reports

Blotski/*Belfast Bulletin*

raised doubts about interrogation techniques, most cartoonists remained cautious about tackling the issue. The corollary was that the themes which provoked a united national response, like anger at IRA bombs in Britain or support for the army, were popular with cartoonists. It was tempting, therefore, to regard events in the province as a struggle between the British virtues of reason, decency and moderation and the Irish antitheses of these, and to depict the army as the epitome of the former.

Thus the cartoons assisted the process of what Philip Elliott called 'social cauterisation' (Elliott, 1976), the binding together of a nation to oppose distasteful developments from outside. The effect was to emphasise the distinction between Northern Ireland and Britain, and to distance Britain from any blame or responsibility for the violent events in the province. Any further analysis of events was redundant: the violence was either the responsibility of the IRA and loyalist paramilitaries, or sprang from inherent Irish racial characteristics.

Licensed Eccentrics: The Cartoonist at Work

Cartooning is a distinctively individual art. While there are strong similarities in the views presented from each setting, it is the skill and style of the individual which attracts the eye—Turner's drollness; Gibbard's neatness; Scarfe's horror; the musings of Cormac. Within the constraints of their publications, the situation is analysed in the end by individuals. What then is the nature of these constraints?

Editorial censorship of cartoonists is rarely explicit. Indeed, cartoonists often deny that they are subjected to any overt political pressure, and claim a high degree of control over the choice and treatment of their themes. Although the selection of cartoon subjects for *Punch* involves a number of people, Mahood, its editorial cartoonist, described the process thus: 'I usually suggest the subject I would like to tackle for my weekly spread'. If there is agreement about this, 'I have complete freedom to do it in whatever way I feel suits me best'.* Cummings, cartoonist for the *Daily Express* and *Sunday Express*, enjoyed a similar independence: although his editors occasionally suggested themes, 'it is usually left to me to decide what subject I want to do and how to do it… I form a view about an event and make my own personal comment'.*

In Ireland the process is slightly different, but the effect is much the same. The higher proportion of freelance cartoonists potentially increases editorial

* Correspondence with the author, October 25 1981 and November 20 1981.

opportunities for political control. In fact editorial sensibilities are more often raised by religious or social indelicacies than by political deviance. Martyn Turner described how the process applied to him: 'I can do what I like when I like. They never asked me or told me to do anything. They've never turned anything down in questions of political taste. They're more tight on sexual matters but never on politics… If I get something left out it's usually because some sub-editor didn't like it or there wasn't any space because of some church notice' (*In Dublin* March 22 1979).

There are occasional indications that some cartoonists feel constricted by the political affiliations of their newspapers, and send cartoons, sometimes

What's it all about?

A frequent criticism of the news media was their failure to describe Northern Ireland's violence within a coherent analysis. Cartoonists were no exception. Although many of them professed surprise that seventeenth century holy wars could flourish in the twentieth century, there was little dispute that it was in fact a religious conflict. Such antique attitudes were deprecated, but they also provided a useful explanation for otherwise incomprehensible events.

Far from becoming more sophisticated as time passed, this view of the conflict was apparently confirmed by the persistence and intractability of the violence. On the question of blame, too, there was considerable accord among British cartoonists: the roots were firmly planted in Irish

THE HUMAN ZOO

Mahood/*Punch*

under pseudonyms, to *Private Eye* or one of the underground papers. In most cases, however, there is no evidence of such frustration. The political symbiosis between cartoonist and editor, established by the cartoonist's decision to work for that particular publication and the paper's decision to employ him, is usually enough to ensure that serious disagreements are rare.

It is in their use of humour rather than their varying conditions of employment that the differences between individual cartoonists are revealed. Only in Northern Ireland itself has the violence been sufficiently prolonged and persistent to produce an equivalent form of humour to the Blitz humour of the Second World war; thus it is peculiar to populations which have learned

bigotry and intransigence. Even when there was a suggestion, as in Scarfe's cartoon, that some of the blame was shared by Britain, it was laid firmly at the door of earlier British administrations. The present governments may make mistakes, but it was generally conceded that their good intentions were above reasonable suspicion.

So, although it was uncommon for the Irish to be stereotyped as the subnormal brutes so common in nineteenth century cartoons, many of the analyses were implicitly ethnic. They assumed that the violence arose from qualities inherent in the Irish character—aggression, superstition, unreliability and a kind of unthinking death wish. The problem with these diagnoses was that it was difficult to prescribe for them. The disease was terminal. When the patient's future was discussed at all by cartoonists, three main responses were discernable. One was a pious and unconvinced prayer that good sense and decency would prevail; another was to take refuge in humour; but the most heartfelt, though carefully expressed, hope was that Ireland would somehow be towed into the mid-Atlantic and away from British consciences, and quietly scuppered.

Gibbard/*Guardian*

to live among violence, and its tone is dry, cynical and resigned. A more conventional and uninvolved form of humour is evident in the work of Heath, Franklin, Wheeler and other cartoonists working in Britain. Northern Ireland has no special demand on their interest, and joins a number of similar themes to form casual quarries to be mined for their humour; even the grim horror of the 1981 hunger strikes could be treated with flip irreverence by cartoonists in *Private Eye*. Contrast this with the cartoons by supporters of the Provisionals: their tone is deadly serious, and their unwillingness to portray their own soldiers in settings which might be regarded as frivolous explains why so many of their cartoons were sober and ineffective. The

FORCED FEEDING

Trog/*Observer*

situation is too serious for jokes. Even the wit of the ubiquitous Cormac, a skilled cartoonist, excites admiration rather than laughter.

The Functions of Cartoons

Cartoons have been used for propaganda purposes for centuries. English views of the 1641 rising in Ireland were partly conditioned by drawings and engravings of the atrocities which accompanied it, and Cruikshank's illustrations had a similar effect during the 1798 rebellion. Freelance professionals were used by opposing sides during many nineteenth century controversies,

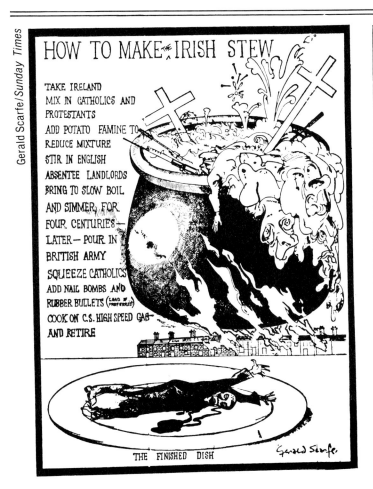

Gerald Scarfe/*Sunday Times*

Mahood/*Punch*

"For Heaven's sake, cut it off and let's enjoy ourselves!"

and bought cartoonists played a major role in the successful campaign against Wilberforce's first Slave Bill (Taylor 1974). Cartoons flourished during both World wars, especially as propaganda for recruitment, and this still applies today.

Nevertheless, on the basis of the Northern Irish experience between 1969 and 1982, propaganda is only one of four main, if overlapping, cartoon categories:

1. The Evangelical Cartoon

This type of cartoon is frankly propagandist, deliberately setting out to present a simple and persuasive explanation of what is happening. Its object is to persuade armchair supporters to become more actively involved—by donating cash or by joining the IRA in the armed struggle, for example—in the cause advocated by the cartoonist. The images are strong, uncomplicated and often crude. Given the limited functions and readership of the activist newspapers in which the majority of these cartoons appeared, it is not surprising that evangelical cartoons are not common. They are mostly Provisional republican, but some have been produced in eastern bloc countries, and in European socialist magazines and newspapers.

2. The Reinforcing Cartoon.

These cartoons are rallying calls to the faithful. Their object is not to attract converts to the cause, but to confirm supporters in the strength of their convictions and generally to boost morale. Unlike most of the evangelical cartoons, the reinforcing cartoons frequently aim to amuse, mainly by ridiculing or discomfiting opponents. They are used in republican newspapers against other non-unionist groups and the British army, but mainly by loyalists in such cartoon strips as 'Bill and Ben the IRA men', and in the 'Taking the Mickey' collections; frequently they are a reaction to propaganda from the other side, and an attempt to counter it.

Humour is not the only means of reinforcing solidarity. One popular theme in republican and loyalist cartoons reminds readers of the sanctions which awaited informers, reinforcing the warning printed in a Provisional newspaper—'Loose talk causes loss of liberty and in many instances can cause death. So keep your knees and keep your head by keeping silent' (*The Vindicator* 3 1973).

3. The Interpretative Cartoon

The form of cartoon closest to other forms of journalism is the editorial cartoon, which appears regularly in many daily newspapers and weekly magazines. Its function is to provide an interpretation of a current news story. There is no reason why these professional cartoonists should have a high commitment to any of the parties in the Northern Irish conflict, although in Europe and North America most conform to a generally liberal position. As a result they more often attack than praise, except when cartoonists think that they have identified a new political light, like William Whitelaw or Bernadette Devlin. Inevitably the love affair turns sour.

Interpretative cartoons provides the largest of the four categories.

4. *The Humorous Cartoon*

It is perhaps surprising that the great majority of cartoons on the Northern Irish conflict are not funny, nor are intended to be. Nevertheless there is a substantial number of cartoons whose sole purpose is to raise a laugh. Irish jokes, for example, often appear in cartoon form, and humorous cartoons about the conflict have appeared in *Punch* and *Private Eye*, even on such unpromising themes as the Hunger Strikes. It is also the predominant view expressed in the cartoons drawn by British soldiers stationed in Northern Ireland. To most soldier cartoonists Northern Ireland represents, at best, an unpopular and inconvenient posting and, at worst, a war which might claim their lives. There is little indication in the cartoons that they understand or care about the issues in dispute, and most of the jokes might just as easily have been printed in army newspapers anywhere in the world.

This is not to suggest that cartoons from the other three categories are not intended to amuse. In this case, however, it is the sole objective.

So it is clear that the functions of cartoons vary considerably and are essentially the products of the setting from which they emerge. One factor predominates above all others: the commitment of the cartoonist to one of the groups engaged in the conflict will determine the category to which his cartoons belong. The greater the bias of the cartoonist, the more likely are the cartoons to be propagandist. The converse is also true: the greater the cartoonist's commitment to a cause, the less likely are the cartoons to be humorous.

Polemics and humour are not comfortable bedfellows. Deep involvement often produces effective propaganda, but rarely humour.

Bibliography

Gustave de Beaumont, *L'Irlande Social, Politique et Religieuse*, Paris 1839

B. Blackbeard and M. Williams (eds), *The Smithsonian Collection of Newspaper Comics*, N.Y., Harry Abrams 1977

T. Blaisdell and P. Selz (eds), *The American Presidency in Political Cartoons*, Berkeley, University Art Museum 1976

E. Bogardus, 'Sociology of the Cartoon', *Sociology and Social Research* 30, 11, 1945

British Army Cartoonists, *By'eeeee the Right... Laugh*, Belfast, Century Services 1973

——, *The Visor Book of Cartoons*, Belfast, Century Services 1977

C. Brooks (ed.), *Best Editorial Cartoons*, L.A., Pelican Publishing, Published annually since 1972

Roy Carr, *Irish Stew*, Exeter, Optima Graphic, No Date

Daniel Casey and Robert Rhodes (eds), *Views of the Irish Peasantry 1800–1916*, Hamden, Archon Books 1977

H. S. Constable, *Ireland from one or two neglected points of view*, London, The Liberty Review Publishing Company 1898

Cormac, *Cormac Strikes Back: Resistance Cartoons from the North of Ireland*, London, Information on Ireland 1982

L. Perry Curtis, Jr., *Apes and Angels: The Irishman in Victorian Caricature*, Newton Abbot, David and Charles 1971

Liz Curtis, 'Echoes of the Past', *The British Press in Ireland*, Information on Ireland, London 1978

Liz Curtis and Alastair Renwick, 'Have you heard the one about... anti-Irish jokes?', *Socialist Challenge*, March 9 1978

Mary Davies, *The Role of the Press in the Recent Northern Ireland Crisis*, Dissertation, University of London 1970

Harry Dickinson, 'A Good Line in Satire', *Times Higher Education Supplement*, December 4 1981

Daniel Dorrity, 'Monkeys in a Menagerie', *Eire–Ireland* 12, 1977

Roger Doyle, 'Drawing for a living', *In Dublin* 73, March/April 1979

Drawn and Quartered 1920–1970, London, Times Newspapers Ltd 1970;
    Preface by Carl Giles; Introduction by Osbert Lancaster

Fifteen Years of Dublin Opinion, Dublin Opinion 1937

Philip Elliott, *The English Press and Northern Ireland*, Typescript 1976

Sigmund Freud, *Basic Writings of Sigmund Freud*, N.Y., The Modern Library
    1974

Rowel Friers, *Riotous Living*, Belfast, Blackstaff Press 1971

——, *Pig in the Parlour*, Belfast, Blackstaff Press 1972

——, *The Book of Friers*, Belfast, Blackstaff Press 1973

——, *The Revolting Irish*, Belfast, Blackstaff Press 1974

John Geipel, *The Cartoon*, Newton Abbot, David and Charles 1972

Carl Giles, see *Drawn and Quartered*

A. Hardcastle, 'The Canterbury Cartoons', *Punch*, November 12 1975

Randall Harrison, *The Cartoon: Communication to the Quick*, California,
    Sage 1981

Paul Hartman and Charles Husband, 'The Press and Prejudice', *Sunday Times*,
    January 27 1974

S. Hess and M. Kaplan, *The Ungentlemanly Art: A History of American Politi-
    cal Cartoons*, N.Y., Macmillan 1975

William Hewison, *The Cartoon Connection*, London, Elm Tree 1977

S. Hoff, *Editorial and Political Cartooning*, N.Y., Stravon Educational Press
    1976

Simon Hoggart, 'The Army PR Men of Northern Ireland', *New Society*, October
    11 1973

Raphael Holinshed et al., *Chronicles*, London 1577

Frank Huggett, *Victorian England as seen by Punch*, London, Sidgwick and
    Jackson 1978

John Kirkaldy, 'Irish Jokes: No Cause for Laughter', *Irish Studies in Britain* 2,
    Autumn–Winter 1981

——, 'English Cartoonists: Ulster Realities', *Eire–Ireland* 1981

Osbert Lancaster, see *Drawn and Quartered*

Richard Ned Lebow, *White Britain and Black Ireland*, Philadelphia, Institute
    for the Study of Human Issues 1976

Belinda Loftus, 'Laughter and Violence: The Northern Cartoonists', *Hibernia*,
    November 28 1975, and resulting correspondence.

Eamonn McCann, *The British Press and Northern Ireland*, London, Northern
    Ireland Socialist Research Centre 1971

Nicholas Mansergh, *The Irish Question*, London, Unwin University Books 1965

K. Meyer et al., 'Women in July Fourth Cartoons: A 100-year Look', *Journal of Communication* 30, 1, 1980

Sarah Nelson, 'Joke Irish', *Fortnight* December 19 1975

——. 'Did you hear the one about the Englishman...', *Fortnight*, January 9 1976

Newsweek, 'The Finer Art of Politics', October 13 1980

Kevin O'Connor, *The Irish in Britain*, London, Sidgwick and Jackson 1972

Oisin, *A Selection of Cartoons by Oisin*, Belfast, Print Workshop 1975

People's Comix, Belfast, Siopa an Phobail, Occasional

George Perry and Alan Aldridge, *The Penguin Book of Comics*, London, Penguin 1971

R. G. G. Price, 'The Irish: *Punch* and the Near West', *Punch*, January 6 1971

D. B. Quinn, *The Elizabethan Age and the Irish*, Cornell, Cornell University Press 1966

R. B. Rajski (ed.), *A Nation Grieved: The Kennedy Assassination in Editorial Cartoons*, Vermont, Charles E. Tuttle 1967

Resistance Comix, Belfast, Siopa an Phobail, Occasional

Ronald Searle, *Ronald Searle*, London, Deutsch 1978

Billy Simpson, 'There is something funny about the Ulster people', *Belfast Telegraph*, May 29 1979

Clifford Smyth, *Rome—Our Enemy* (Pamphlet), Belfast 1973

Richard Stives, *A Hair of the Dog: Irish Drinking and American Stereotype*, Pennsylvania, University Park 1977

Robert Taylor, 'Images of the Irish', *New Society*, November 28 1974

Martyn Turner, 'Men, Dogs and Pigs', *Fortnight*, July 4 1972

A. F. Westin (ed.), *Getting Angry six times a week*, Boston, Beacon Press 1979

M. E. Wheeler and S. K. Reed, 'Response to before and after Watergate caricature', *Journalism Quarterly* 52, 1975

Michael Wynn Jones, 'Cummings and his Press', *Spectator*, October 30 1971